DREAMS AND REALITIES OF RURAL DEVELOPMENT IN INDIA

DREAMS AND REALITIES OF RURAL DEVELOPMENT IN INDIA

BY

DR. VIJAY PRAKASH SHARMA

KALPAZ

First Published, 2018

Published by

Kalpaz Publications
C-30, Satyawati Nagar,
Delhi – 110052
Ph.: 011-47034999, 9811692060
www.kalpazpublications.com
E-mail: kalpaz@hotmail.com

Printed at: G. Print Process, Delhi

Cataloging in Publication Data—DK
Courtesy: D.K. Agencies (P) Ltd. <docinfo@dkagencies.com>

Sharma, Vijay Prakash, 1954- **author.**
Dreams and realities of rural development in India / by Dr. Vijay Prakash Sharma.
pages cm
Includes bibliographical references.
ISBN 9789386397959 (HB)

1. Rural development—India—Jharkhand. 2. Tribes—India—Jharkhand—Economic conditions. I. Title.

LCC HN690.Z9C6 2018 | DDC 307.14120954127 23

Contents

Preface

India is a country with approximately 80% population living in the villages. It is therefore, important to develop the villages then only the country can be considered as developed country in the international arena. Tribal are integral part of Indian villages therefore, integrated village development model is being suggested here for integrated tribal /rural development.

While Teaching M.A. Rural Development course in Ranchi University, I felt that students and teachers are running from pillars to post in search of reference materials. Looking at their plight, I decided to present a collection of relevant study and teaching materials for students and teachers in rural development.

Rural and tribal development is much hailed dimensions of India's development after independence. The dream of constitution designers that every Indian citizen should have right of equality and for this, they provided special protection to the weaker sections of the society majority of whom lives in rural India. To achieve this noble goal, they designed modus operandi for their development through various constitutional provisions, laid down the principles of protective discrimination that operates particularly in matters of reservation of seats in legislators, educational institutions, and government services.

The materials included in this volume are collection of Research papers presented by the author in different National and International seminars in last two years. Even then, some references inadvertently left out to be mentioned may be due to human memory error for which I seek your moral support to pardon.

This book is an outcome of my sincere effort in presenting this introductory volume to the student readers to help them understand the subject.

Vijay Prakash Sharma

Preface

Chapter - 1

Dreams and Realities of Rural Development in India

Rural and tribal development is much hailed dimensions of India's development after independence. The dream of constitution designers that every Indian citizen should have right of equality and for this, they provided special protection to the weaker sections of the society majority of whom lives in rural India. To achieve this noble goal, they designed modus*operandi* for their development through various constitutional provisions, laid down the principles of protective discrimination that operates particularly in matters of reservation of seats in legislators, educational institutions, and government services. The Vth and VIth schedules of the constitution of India also included under the orbit of protective discrimination. The Vth schedule enables the Union of India to provide guidance to the state in the matter of the administration of the areas covered by the schedules, beside it enables the Governor of state to promulgate regulations and to with holds application of any legislation in notified areas. Among measures of protective discrimination particular mention is also made of legislations restricting alienation of tribal lands. Directive principles of state policy incorporated in the constitution of India require that the state to take measures for the welfare of the disadvantaged sections particularly scheduled tribes and scheduled castes. This was the dream of the constitution makers and to fulfill the dream, inputs were provided by the government for development through five year plans.

Development has been key word in the post second world war period. Defining the concept of development in 1962 the UnitedNations Secretary

General said, "Development is growth plus change, change in turn is social and cultural as well as qualitative." Since then the concept of development has been much debated. So development in a technical sense refers to qualitative and structural changes in the state of economy. For some people, it also refers to relatively stable long range increase in real income that is accompanied by a change in institutional set up, production technique and world view. The dominant paradigm of development until the mid 1970's centered round the rate of economic growth that still persists. Scholars are of opinion that the green revolution of mid- sixties have made differential impact on the development of agriculture among the region which in turn have influenced the inter-regional differences in the incidence of poverty. The entire process of development has been weighted in favour of rich and affluent. The share of the poor has been nominal. Unrealized utopia has led to widening disparity in rural society.

Rural: As per the Webster's dictionary rural means "open land" and according to the United States census rural includes all persons living outside urban area and who live on farm. Agriculture is generally the main occupation in rural areas.

The very concept of rural development requires some elaboration. According to UNESCO, rural development is a process through which a series of quantitative and qualitative changes are brought about in rural areas for improved living conditions.

Rural development: can be defined in several ways but for all practical purposes it means helping the poor people living in the villages in their economic development. The major objectives of the rural development programs are:

- To achieve enhanced production and productivity in the rural areas
- To bring about a greater socio-economic equity
- To bring about a spatial balance in social and economic development
- To bring about improvement in the ecological environment so that it may be conducive to growth and happiness, and
- To develop broad based community participation in the process of development

Main Lines of Activity

The activities considered important for rural development can be divided into the Agricultureand related matters, Irrigation, Communications, Education, Health, Supplementary employment, Housing, Training and Social Welfare.

1. Agriculture and related matters: The programme includes reclamation of available virgin and waste land, provision of commercial fertilizers and improved seeds, promotion of fruit and vegetable cultivation, improved agricultural technique, supply of technical information, improved agricultural implements, improved marketing and credit facilities, provision of soil surveys and prevention of soil erosion, encouragement of the use of natural and compost manures and improvement of livestock.
2. Irrigation: The programme include provision of water for agriculture through minorirrigation works, e.g., tanks, canals, surface wells, tube-wells, etc., the intention beingthat the agricultural lands be served with irrigation facilities.
3. Communications: The road system on the countryside to be developed to link everyvillage up to a maximum distance of half a mile by feeder roads through voluntarylabour of the villagers themselves. Roads to be provided for, and maintained by the State or other public agencies.
4. Education: The community projects to provide for social education, expansion andimprovement of primary and secondary education. Vocational and technical training be emphasized in all the stages of the educational programme.
5. Health: The Health Organisation to provide primary health in the Development Blocks and a secondary health unit equipped with a hospital and a mobile dispensary at the headquarters of the Project area and serving the area as a whole.
6. Supplementary Employment: The unemployed and the under-employed persons in the village community be provided with gainful employment to such extent as is possible, by the development of cottage and small-scale industries, construction of brick kilns and saw mills and encouragement of employment through participation in the tertiary sector of the economy.
7. Housing: Apart from the provision of housing under various schemes, provide demonstration and training in improved techniques and designs for rural housing.

8. Training: The training of farmers, village level workers, project supervisors and other personnel to be carried out for skill up-gradation and enhanced efficiencies.
9. Social welfare: Make provision for audio-visual aid for instruction and recreation, for organizations of community entertainment, sports activities and Melas.

The rural development in India is expected through the initiative of external change-agents and outside resources, with the mutual involvement of the rural population. The external forces or resources can be useful to the extent of people's participation and, thus, rural development is a people's programme. The external agencies should phase out when villagers are educationally and economically advanced to carry on their own.

In general, it seems that the goal of rural development in India is eradication of poverty and unemployment which are the major twin causes of rural - poverty in India. All most all government programmes, (baring a few), are targeted in this direction but lack of proper implementation poses a big question mark.

Eradication of rural poverty is possible only by generation of income and employment opportunities for the rural poor especially for those who are at the lowest rung of the social order. Somehow, our modern development planners ignored employment and skill development potential inbuilt in our village jajmani system since time immemorial. It is important to emphasize here that certainamount of diversification in the occupational opportunities available in the rural areas, have to be revived in non-farm sector as it has still many openings for absorbing a large number of rural people by inculcating in them the requisite skills in the context of emerging trades and demands.

Most people in rural and tribal areas are engaged in their traditional occupations which are land and forest based and therefore, had developed an orientation to think of their occupational life in terms of interaction with land and what so ever it can produce. In view of the constraints of providing land to a large number of landless people, certain attempts have to be made to create employment opportunities in non-land based occupations, mostly in small-scale, cottage and household industries. In the new strategies of development, the role of education as instrument of socio-economic-transformation has become more important. The symbiotic relationship between education and rural economy is now being appreciated by policy makers and planners.

The emerging concept of development lays emphasis on people's participation which is a welcome departure from the yore of imperial rule. The role of education has been re-examined in the process of nation development. Education has been considered important source for developing human potentialities, increasing production and nations overall development. Kothari commission of education (1964-66) has recommended that there should be educational revolution and radical reform through internal transformation of the system of education so as to relate education to life's need and aspiration of the nation, but a lot has to be done in this area. Educational Institutions like universities can contribute a lot for rural development planning and implementation. For any machinery to work effectively, it needs to be placed in well trained hands. This becomes even more crucial in programme implementation initiative. Some of when it is about governance machinery. The village governance initiative should aim to facilitate smooth functioning of Panchayati Raj Institutions and empowering grass root leadership. This should be done by training various stakeholders of village society through workshops and seminars.

The idea is to help stakeholders get a perspective on various issues and help them in getting clarity about their roles and responsibilities. This should be done to build responsible and accountable leadership capacities at the grassroots level. Thousands have been deprived of benefits from NRGEA because of the present haphazard rural development the issues that people should be sensitized as part of this programme about government schemes ,participatory planning, empowerment, communication skills, leadership skills, gender issues, stress management, social audit, Right to Information .

Understanding the people

Universities can help in Poverty focused development strategies. Can work only if planners try and understand the people for whom they plan development. It is not enough to produce plans, which look excellent on paper. Plans designed to assist development of the poor people must take account of their needs, and their capacity to absorb benefits from the development process. Most plan failures can be attributed not to technical imperfections in their formulation, but usually to a lack of understanding of socio – cultural realities on the part of both planners and project administrators. Here anthropology have great role to play.

The university has vast human resource to help the villagers in –

1. Awareness generation about various government programmes

2. Participatory planning as there are specialized departments like rural development/ anthropology and sociology.
3. In addition to this NSS volunteers can contribute for the same.
4. Training of newly elected PRI functionaries in maintaining books of account by commerce students.
5. Decentralized Planning: Bottom to top approach.
6. People's participation in formulation of plans, prioritizing the plans and their execution.
7. To provide quick solution for ecological & especially soil development & control on soil evasion due to excessive mining & industrialization-
8. The responsibility of education on socially useful productive work can be given to the local farmers and artisans and not to teachers on specific formal subjects. At the same time, music, art & sports should be given the privilege of a formal subject and should be included in the syllabus.
9. Autonomous institutions can be developed for development of the children in different aspects like tribal culture, language, sports etc.
10. Structured facilities for sports can be made available in the district/village level. Special attention should be given to sports, like men's & women's hockey, Archery, Athletics, race, Kabaddi etc. to promote interest in these sports among the children.

Till now, a few towns have been selected in the name of developmental plans, but for this, the villagers had to pay the price. The resources of the villagers were exploited in a colonized manner. The actual development rate which was required to solve the problems of poverty, unemployment, migration, displacement while, catering to the primary objectives of rural development, was very slow. The regional development based on reckless exploitation of natural resources, individual development pressurized by the Block offices, makes the problems more complicated. The different developmental plans were made in the State Capitals, thus neglecting the geographical, demographical, and ecological differences, for which specific plans and projects could not be formulated. The policy makers did not pay much attention to the special characteristics of the rural society, like attachment of the community to the nature, forests; laborious life, easy satisfaction etc. and thus their representation & participation in planning was diverted to wrong directions. On the contrary, the key to policy making for development should be based on people's participation in the process of continuous social development.

The following recent studies and publications clearly reflect the contemporary rural situation in various states of India.

Dr. P Purushotham (2015) in his article entitled, Tribal Livelihood Issues: Observations from an Empirical Study in Some North Indian States" shared his observations from an empirical study in some north Indian states on tribal livelihood issues confirms that there is an urgent need to rejuvenate the delivery system. The development functionaries must be motivated to visit the villages regularly and deliver the development services to the poor. For this to hap-pen, the primary stakeholders must be organized into pressure groups to demand their legiti-mate entitlements from the state machinery. The local resource base of these villages needs to be strengthened, recharged and nurtured so as to provide dependable livelihood security to the poor. The new dry land farm technologies, such as drip irrigation, seed replacement, moisture conservation, application of bio fertilizers and pesticides, etc. offer a vast scope for strengthening the livelihood base of the people here. To operationalise this, the households should be organized, and their awareness levels increased. In this regard, the way the tribal households were educated about their rights to forest produce, and exposed to the range of technologies available to them in tendu leaf collectors of Mendha Lekha gram sabha in Gadchiroli, Maharastra in 2011 is noteworthy. After three years of struggle, these households got the rights to collect, transport and sell bamboo, setting a trend. The gaping holes in the implementation of the FRA, very common in the villages studied, can only be filled by the involvement of civil society at all levels.

Dr Shankar Chatterjee (2015) in his article entitled, "Development of Scheduled Tribe in India: Facts with Field Cases" opines that, ST people staying in rural areas require more on education, awareness building camp, and Government support. For example, *Chenchus* were not aware about institutional health facilities; moreover necessary arrangement was not initiated to rectify the hand pump/ irrigation pump. Local human resources may be utilized in this re-gard for the benefit of dwellers. Education has to be given emphasis because in the absence of education and wisdom they might be exploited by others. In case of ST people of *Bankura*, it was observed that because of lack of education many families were deprived of Government Scheme. So massive awareness campaign may be initiated and if require NGO may be drafted for this. Moreover it has to be admitted that in both the states politically they were not organized like other community as sequel economic development was not impressive.

Dr. Debashis Debnath (2015) in his article entitled, “The Role of Indigenous Knowledge system in Biodiversity management and Livelihood Securities in the Baigas of Madhya Pradesh: An Anthropological Perspective” observes that the indigenous peoples applied the indigen-ous knowledge for conservation and utilization of various non-timber species for their surviv-al and livelihoods. But in the implementation of participatory forestry, the basic objectives of conservation of the bio-resources and species diversities viz. collection and conservation of the non-timber forest products including medicinal plants, participatory silvi-culture, processing, value addition and local market development were not given due importance to that extent as required. One method of forest conservation by them is through social traditions. Various parts of their bio-diversities are used in their life-cycle rituals. The sacred groves are found in them which have the areas protected, preserved and conserved with reli-gious affiliation and having varied species conserved for different utility and purposes. There are some temples which have the trees protected, preserved and conserved with religious affiliation for conservation of various species. In them a number of taboos observed in the trees like Sal among. A number of sacred water resources under different are observed in them. There are ample scopes to enhance their income sources from the forest products as they are living in the fringe forest villages and are depending to the large extent on collections of fuel wood, fodder, NTFPs including medicinal plants, cattle grazing and marketing of the raw products at the nominal price in the local market. Moving away from the income or consump-tion criteria the poverty has been equated with help of livelihood security. In the Baigas the people have attempted to livelihood security by producing some products. For instance, in the Baigas they produce broom of chhind, rope of mova grass, honey, mahua liquor and mohua oil. All of them they produce in their traditional skills with locally available raw materials.

Dr.Pradip K. Bhowmick(2015) in his article “Empowering the tribal communities through conservation & cultivation of commercially valuable medicinal & aromatic plants: an action research”, tried to explore the scope of getting economic benefit from the cultivation, conservation and selling of medicinal and aromatic plants in three tribal settings viz. Kharia, Bhumij and Santhals of West Bengal and came to conclusion that the agro-climatic specifica-tions existent in these two studied blocks indicate bigger prospect of captive plantation in re-spect of some high value species of medicinal & aromatic plants. Dr Shankar Chatterjee and Dr (Ms) N. Kalpalatha (2015) in their article entitled, “SHGs at “Take-off” Stage for Development of Rural Minorities in India: Field Observations” has observed that, With the implementation of SGSY by emphasizing on Self-help Group, it was expected that huge number of families would come out of poverty as SGSY was implemented with lot of hope, hype and hoopla. The reason was simple as different rounds of concurrent evaluation studies on IRDP carried out by the Ministry of Rural Development, Government of India reveal that IRDP and its allied five programmes could not make much dent to eradicate poverty from the country. Accordingly SGSY was launched from 1st April, 1999 by merging IRDP and other 5 five programmes. However, there were some shortcomings in implementation of SGSY and based on Prof. R. *Radhakrishna* Committee SGSY has been re-structured as NRLM. Only time can say impact of NRLM to eradicate poverty. Thus it is evident that under the umbrella of SHG, beneficiaries have been benefitted both economically and socially.

Dr. Vijay Prakah Sharma (2015) in his articlethinkingabout Rural Development through Integrated Village Development Model in Jharkhand opines thatsince the independence of India, much is being done in the name of Rural/ Tribal development to bring these millions of people in the mainstream of the advanced and modern cultural groups. Irrigation facilities were created for development of agriculture in 3rd and 4th five year plans and also completed by the government Development represents an increase in the capacities of the society to organize for its own objectives and to carry out its programmes more effectively. India is a country with 80% population living in the villages. It is therefore, important to develop the villages then only the country can be considered as developed country in the international arena. Tribal are integral part of Indian villages therefore, village development model is suggested for integrated tribal development. The 5th schedule of the constitution was paternalistic while the 6th schedule granted autonomy to the tribal. Considering all the above he suggests that a ***village level integrated rural development model*** should be considered for implementing the rural/tribal development plan as most of the strategies failed due to lack of integrated approach.

Finally, rural development should lead to improvement with respect to the followings-

(a) Agricultural productivity per hectare of land and poor labour

(b) Employment of educated and uneducated in rural areas reviving village Jajmani system approach

(c) Distribution of income and wealth including land ownership

(d) Decentralization of political power at village level and people's participation in decision making

(e) Horizontal as well as vertical mobility of labour

(f) Welfare measures to suit the needs

(g) Value belief and attitude.

Above all, one may add that development of social consciousness, sense of pride, process of collectivization and development of leadership should also be important element of rural development. The forces of globalization has entered in rural areas hence the government must be cautious in dealing with FDI investments in rural areas.

References

1. Bhowmick, Pradip K. 2015Empowering the tribal communities through conservation & cultivation of commercially valuable medicinal & aromatic plants: an action research in Vijay Prakash Sharma edited book Contemporary Indian Society(In the beginning of 21st Century), Anmol Publications Private Ltd., New Delhi.
2. Chatterjee. Shankar,2015 Development of Scheduled Tribe in India: Facts with Field Cases, in Vijay Prakash Sharma edited book Contemporary Indian Society(In the beginning of 21st Century), Anmol Publications Private Ltd., New Delhi.
3. Chatterjee. Shankar, 2015 Rural development Programmes in India, RBSA Publishers, Jaipur.
4. Chatterjee. Shankar and N. Kalpalatha, 2015 SHGs at "Take-off" Stage for Development of Rural Minorities in India: Field Observations, in Vijay Prakash Sharma edited book Contemporary Indian Society(In the beginning of 21st Century), Anmol Publications Private Ltd., New Delhi.
5. Debnath. Debashis, 2015 The Role of Indigenous Knowledge system in Biodiversity management and Livelihood Securities in the Baigas of Madhya Pradesh: An Anthropological Perspective in Vijay Prakash Sharma edited book Contemporary Indian Society(In the beginning of 21st Century), Anmol Publications Private Ltd., New Delhi.
6. Purushotham, P. 2015 Tribal Livelihood Issues: Observations from an Empirical Study in Some North Indian States- in Vijay Prakash Sharma edited book Contemporary Indian Society(In the beginning of 21st Century), Anmol Publications Private Ltd., New Delhi.
7. Sharma. Vijay Prakash, 2015 Status of Flagship Programme *Janani Suraksha Yojna* In Rural India, in Vijay Prakash Sharma edited bookContemporary Indian Society(In the beginning of 21st Century), Anmol Publications Private Ltd., New Delhi.
8. Sharma. Vijay Prakash 2015 Tribal Society And Unrest: A Case of Naxal Affected Jharkhand, B.M. Mukherjee and Mollick edited book Tribal Unrest In Middle India.

9. Sharma. Vijay Prakash and B.M. Mukherjee, 2014 Need for Water and Land Resources among Tribe of Central India, published in B.M. Mukherjee edited book" Tribal People of Central India", K K PUBLICATIONS New Delhi.
10. Sharma. Vijay Prakash, 2014 Tribal Health in India-An Overview, D K Behera Edited book, Contemporary Society, Vol. ix, Concept Publishing Company, New Delhi.
11. Sharma. Vijay Prakash, 2014 Thinking about Tribal Development through Integrated Village Development Model in Jharkhand, in P. Dash Sharma edited book Livelihood and Health, Serial Publication, New Delhi,
12. Sharma. Vijay Prakash, 2013 Promoting Institutional deliveries In Tribal areas: The Role of Janani *Suraksha Yojna(JSY),* Journal of Social Research, Department of Anthropology, Ranchi University, Ranchi, Vol.36-39; N0-1-2,PP-46-52,(ISSN 0449-315X),March.

Chapter - 2

Indigenous Health Care Systems: A case study of Traditional Healers and Tribal Vaidyas

The Tribal Vaidyas are found among most of the tribal communities of Jharkhand who are practicing traditional healing system since time immemorial but now a days are being ignored. There were abundant sources of medical knowhow in the subcontinent. Healing is practiced by people from all levels of society who live and work in intimate relation with their environment. They range from home remedies related to nutrition and treatment for minor illnesses, to more sophisticated procedures such as midwifery, bone setting and treatment of snake bites and mental disorders. There were also specialists in bloodletting, experts in physical medical practices and others with intimate knowledge of medicinal plants. All these areas of folk practices have their particular folklore that preserved and transmitted such knowledge. Some healing practices were considered to be sacred and were associated with rituals that helped safeguard them. It is interesting to note that in folk traditions there is considerable overlap between healing plants and sacred plants, and certain healing plants were venerated even before medical knowledge was codified into the canonical texts of Ayurveda.

Indigenous health system and Tribal Vaidyas

Tribal Vaidyas among Munda Community of Jharkhand, practice their own indigenous health system since time immemorial that keeps them healthy. They have expertise in conservation, collection and use of different medicinal plants, their parts such as roots, stems, skins, flowers, leaves, and even the whole plant in the treatment of health complications such as Epilepsy, diabetes, Arthritis, Jaundice, Fever, Cough and Cold, weaknesses, Diarhorea, Hematoria, Sinusitis, worm, wounds, Eye redness, regulation of menses, acne, Toothache, Headache, Earache and skin diseases etc. Taken together, the Munda Vaidyas treat 33 types of health problems.

Rural or tribal area is situated at difficult terrain to reach by modern medical practitioners so there is an opportunity for tribal Vaidyas to continue their indigenous health system for peoples benefit but for this, they need government recognition and financial assistance to survive. Modern medical system is too costly to be adopted by the tribal people so Tribal Vaidyas are the only alternative. They are revered by their people and enjoy their faith in the old health system. The processing of medicine for use is also simple and time tested, can be easily prepared at home. This indigenous health system is backed by faith healing system of tribal GUNIS, OJHAS and SOKHAS. They have many success stories in treatment of chronic and simple diseases though they lack the scholarly aura, many which specialize in specific healing practices are held in high esteem. For example, it is not uncommon for scholarly Ashtavaidyas of Kerala to seek the help of folk healers in pediatric care, poison therapy or diseases of the mind. Classical Ayurveda has been enriched over centuries through such interactions and exchange with regional folk practices.

Even before medical knowledge was codified into the canonical texts of Ayurved, there were abundant sources of medical knowledge in the subcontinent. Ayurved is probably the most documented Indigenous medical system that emerged from folk tradition of health care in India. Even though during the British colonial period official status of Ayurveda and other traditional healing systems were relegated to secondary roles and western medicine became dominant, Ayurvedic colleges offering diplomas were created and the study of classical texts in Sanskrit were initiated in many centers around India. Many of these institutions integrated Ayurveda education with biomedical education curriculum and western concepts of disease and wellness. Pharmaceutical companies also began to manufacture Ayurvedic and other forms of traditional medicines on a large scale to deal with the diminished capability of practitioners and patients to make medical preparations.

After Independence, the government of India made efforts to recognize Ayurveda, Siddha and Unani as being on par with allopathic biomedicine. In 1964 a government body for setting norms for the manufacture and the control of the quality of traditional medicinal preparations was formed.

In 1970 the government of India passed the Indian Medical Central Council Act to standardize Ayurvedic teaching institutions, their curriculum and their diplomas. More recently the government created the Deparment of AYUSH (Department of Ayurveda, Yoga & Naturopathy, Unani, Siddha and Homoeopathy) to support research and development of traditional medicine, and to set standards and regulate the activities related to practice but neglected tribal system of health care Hodopathy.

Today the general trend is to comply with the norms of modern biomedicine. In traditional medical schools the vocabulary and diagnostic tools of modern medicine are replacing traditional terms, and techniques and students are increasingly becoming unfamiliar with classical references and methodologies.

In the last few decades there has been growing interest in alternative forms of therapy globally. In addition, attempts by devotees of New Age culture to ascribe new layers of meaning to the concepts of Ayurveda have propagated a simplified and modified version of Ayurvedic culture and practice. While this has stimulated the development of tourism for well-being, leisure Ayurveda, in India, with spas and hotels offering different kinds of simplified treatments, for many in India and abroad these commercialized variants have come to represent Ayurveda.

There are attempts by biomedical and Ayurvedic researchers to correlate Ayurvedic understanding of the nature of disease with modern biomedical concepts. The materia medica of Ayurveda has attracted the attention of researchers and commercial concerns in India and abroad interested in identifying active molecules and manufacturing commercial versions of traditional formulations. These novel demands along with renewed popularity traditional medical practices within India itself have created conflicting conditions for traditional medicine in general and for Ayurveda in particular.

The hereditary Tribal Vaidyas (physicians of Jharkhand) are among the small group of traditional medical practitioners who have endeavored to retain the practices of their ancestors. With changing social structure and the norms imposed by the government regulations, Tribal Vaidyas too are striving to adapt their practice to contemporary standards but in vain. The interviews conducted over the last few years by different scholars with the remaining Tribal Vaidyas in different Indian states highlight the issues that traditional medicine faces in such a modern context. Mention may be made of studies in Jharkhand and Bihar by O.P. Upadhyaya (1998),

A.K. Prabhaker and S.P. Roy (2000), Prashant Mishra (2003), P. Kumari (2006), M.C.Mahanta (2007), A.K. Haldar (2008), I.P. Gupta (2009), A.K. Mairh (2010). These studies are important contributions in understanding Indigenous Health system of Jharkhand and Bihar.

Problems of Tribal or indigenous health system

The dominance of modern business oriented health system, Tribal or indigenous health system is facing a lot of problems.

(a) Indigenous health system in tribal area is neglect by the government.

(b) Tribal Vaidyas are left with poor earnings, hence having poor economic condition.

(c) Tribal Vaidyas are generally less educated or illiterate having expertise in oral and visual identification of medicinal plants and their use and are unable to document the process.

(d) New generation is list bothered to adopt this system.

(e) Deforestation is destroying the local medicinal plants used by them.

The Tribal Vaidyas are found among most of the tribal communities of Jharkhand who are practicing traditional healing system since time immemorial but now a days are being ignored. In the light of above background, the question is **what we need to do?**

I. We need to open two fronts for our action- 1. Field centered activities i.e. opening and running the centers and

II. Think tank activities like policy level advocacy and demystification of the advertised idea that "allopath is the only way to cure modern world health complications"

Suggestions

We need to choose priorities and our actions out of alternatives suggested here or develop a new alternative.

1. Promote traditional healing centers with local help.
2. Promote traditional healers (Tribal Vaidyas) and enrich their knowledge.
3. Introduce certification course for traditional healers (Tribal Vaidyas).
4. Work as pressure group to advocate with government to adopt a policy and legally recognize traditional healers (Tribal Vaidyas).

5. Documenting Tribal Vaidyas knowledge for their skill building (not for market moguls).
6. Establish a forum at national level for policy discussion and promotion of traditional healers (Tribal Vaidyas).
7. Initiate academic dialogue to fight exploitation of Tribal Vaidyas by modern market forces.

References

1. A summary of interviews with the Asthavaidya and observations is given in the paper below-http://www.jaim.in/article.asp?issn=0975-9476; year=2010; volume=1; issue=4; spage=245; epage=250; aulast=Menon.
2. Sharma, V.P. Community Health Care with Alternative medicines, Seminar paper, SADED, Rajendra Bhawan, New Delhi, 15th July, 2016.
3. Sharma, V.P. *SWASTHYA RAKSHA HETU SAMUHIK SWASTHYA- EK VIKALP*, Seminar paper, SADED, Rajendra Bhawan, New Delhi, 15th July, 2016.
4. Sharma, V.P. Regional folk practices of traditional healing among Tribal, Seminar paper, SADED and SHRAMJIVI UNNAYAN, Goberghoosi, Jharkhand, 25th-26th September, 2016.
5. Upinder Singh, Nayanjot Lahiri, Ancient India: New Research, Oxford University Press, India 2010.
6. Zysk, K. Medicine in the Veda: Religious healing in the Veda, Motilal Banarisidas, Delhi 1996.
7. Zysk, K. Asceticism and Healing in Ancient India: Medicine in The Buddhist Monastery, Motilal Banarisidas, Delhi 1998.

Chapter –3

Cultural Traits of Rural Jharkhand

Cultural trait- A cultural trait is a learned behavior of values, traditions, symbols and meaning that are passed from one generation to another within specific community of people. These cultural traits are learned, transmitted, based on symbols, changeable, integrated, ethnocentric and adaptive. The cultural traits represent Cultural identity of a people.

Cultural identity is the identity or feeling of belonging to a group. It is part of a person's self conception and self perception and is related to nationality, ethnicity, religion, social group that has its own distinct culture. In this way, a cultural trait is both characteristics of the individual but also of the culturally identical group of members sharing the same cultural traits (Ennaji 2005,19-25).

Before we discuss the cultural traits of Jharkhand, we need to know what culture is. Anthropologists consider culture as abstract values, beliefs, and perception of the world that lie behind people's behavior, and which that behavior reflects. These are shared by the members of the society, and when acted upon they produce behavior considered acceptable within that society. Cultures are learned through the medium of language, rather than inherited biologically, and parts of culture function as an integrated whole (Havilland 1981, 26).

Culture is based on symbols. Leslie White considered that all human behavior originates in the use of symbols. Art, religion, and money involve the use of symbols. Most important symbolic aspect of culture is language.

Now let us examine different possible aspects that may represent Cultural trait of Jharkhand.

1. Language: Jharkhand is multi lingual state having people speaking Hindi, Mundari, Kurukh, Santhali, Malto, Nagpuri including sadari or sadani. Khortha and Panch parganiya etc.
2. Religion: Hindu 81%, Muslim 13.8%, Christian 4.1%.

   It seems difficult to select them as cultural traits of Jharkhand.
3. Food is another aspect that creates National to Cultural to Personal identities.

"All distinct cultural, ethnic, and [nations] define themselves, and tend to denigrate others, by asserting the superiority of the foods that represent their social and moral values.

What 'we' eat is good and what 'they' eat is bad. ... meanings associated with specific foods, the ways of preparing and eating them also involve cultural, ethnic, and social class prejudices. At the individual level, eating habits can be quite revealing of personality [traits].

"Food is not just what we eat. It is an expression of who we are, how we live and the world we inhabit" Mark Kurlansky (2007).

"Cultural traits, social institutions, national histories, and individual attitudes cannot be entirely understood without an understanding also of how these have meshed with our varied and particular modes of eating" (*Farb and Amelagos,* 1980, p. 4).

Food is used to strengthen the bonds between individuals, families and communities. For Anthropologists, food and food ways offer unique powerful windows to understand individual cultures and societies, especially when they are situated in the context of global and historical flows and food: the media is flooded with books, articles, television shows, and blogs on internet. Anthropologists in the main are interested in understanding culture and society through objects, words, and behavior. They consider how individual are "localized" in their culture and society. As a member of a particular society, which none the less are always subject to global influence? As a member of a particular society (social group), a person's thoughts, feelings, and behaviours to a large extent are learned from others within that society although culture is never a straight jacket in this respect. Another premise of many anthropologists is that not only meaning but also physical characteristics of an object are culturally construed. Many things are edible, but each culture determines what is considered food. Something may "stink" in one culture but be fragrant in another. Given these two premises, anthropologists study food, its production and consumption in order to understand the culture and society of a people. (Tierney and Tierney 2012).

Local food culture of Jharkhand

Jharkhand was carved out of southern Bihar is home of thirty two tribes. Prominent among them are the Mundas, the earliest tribal settlers in the area. The Santhals are the last of the tribes to settle down here. Hence the people and culture of Jharkhand is drenched in traditions. The tribal people of the state live in villages and are dependent on agriculture to earn their livelihood but since they have not been exposed to modern techniques of farming they follow traditional methods.

Local food of Jharkhand tribe includes vegetarian as well as non-vegetarian dishes. Dal (pulses), rice and vegetable curry, are the staple food of Jharkhand. While rice is the staple, roti (unleavened bread) is also occasionally an important part of main meals. Pulses, vegetables, meat, eggs and fish are eaten with rice or roti. The tribes make their own local liquor called 'hanria', which is made of rice and can taste pungent for first timers! The tribes mainly take boiled cereals, a curry of boiled vegetables or meat or edible roots seasoned with salt and chilies and millet. Among the tribal specialties are "Asur Pitha" (prepared from the flour of Mahua) and "Sauria Ghata" which is cooked like rice with the crushed maize. "Korwa Lata" and "Korwa Jatangi" are also famous among the tribes. The tribes relish a beverage called "Handia" which is prepared by fermenting rice with the help of biro (a medicinal cake), partially cooked over fire in a Handi (earthen cooking pot). Then it is cooked and mixed with powdered biro. Then the pot is kept in a cool place for some days and after a certain time the Handia gets ready to be distributed.

Litti and Chokha are two special delicacies of Jharkhand. People include different kinds of pickle in each meal.

The regular food is tasty and less spicy. People also like different kinds of leafy vegetables such as saag. Panchforan, a blend of five aromatic seeds is used for some of the vegetable dishes. The tribal people of the state often use flowers such as drumstick flowers and jhirool for vegetable preparations. Mutton, chicken as well as fish are used to prepare delectable non-vegetarian cuisines.

The staple food of the tribal is boiled rice, which they eat with cooked pulse popularly known as dal. They use pulses of different kinds which they produce in the kitchen-garden attached to their houses. They all eat goats, sheep, fowls and pigs, but very rarely do they drink milk. They are immensely fond of liquor and they brew a sort of rice-beer commonly known as *Handia* which is said to be highly refreshing and invigorating and has great importance in their religious rites.

Kadhi Bari- these fried soft dumplings made of besan (gram flour) are cooked in spicy gravy of yogurt and besan. It goes well over plain rice.

Khichdi- Mix of Rice, Dal and several Vegetables; steamed together to give a distinctive taste of different ingredients combined in one dish. It is often topped up with ghee.

Ghugni - It is a preparation made of black grams soaked (either lightly/ overnight)in water and then sauced in mustard oil in a wok. All kinds of garam masala made as paste on a sill is used for flavouring and chana is also ground to form a paste used as thickener. This thickens the masala and makes gravy as per desire. After proper seasoning and bhunjana water is added to the mix for gravy as desired.

Pittha - It is something like momos. It could be either salty or sweet. It is either a semi circular/ball shaped preparation made of crust made of soft rice flour and filled with preparations made of Channa Daal lentil paste, or Poppy seeds & Gur (Jaggery). and then steamed in water/ milk (allowed to thicken).

Choora - beaten rice, served with a coat of creamy curd and sugar or jaggery. In winters, this is mildly baked and accompanied with a thick spicy preparation made of peas and onions.

Sattu - powdered baked gram, a high energy giving food usually mixed with water or with milk. Sometimes, sattu mixed with spices is used to prepare stuffed 'chapattis', locally called as 'makuni roti'.

Dhuska - a deep fried item prepared from a mixture of powdered rice and ghee but is salted.

Litti - Powdered baked gram is mixed with chopped onions,green chillies,lemon juice, coriander leaves. This mixture is filled inside atta (flour) and either barbecued over coal or deep fried with oil. Best accompanied with Ghee, Curd and Chokha and baigan bharta.

***SAAGS* (Plant Leaves) of Jharkhand**

Mange saag, Kalmia saag, Gadara saag, Koinar saag, Chakod saag, Sarla saag, Bhench saag, Chimti saag, Katai saag, Dhhahdhhaa saag, Golgola saag, Khesaari saag (Lathyrus sativus):, Poi saag (Basella alba), Palak Saag (Spinach) Bathua Saag (Chenopodium album), Methi Saag (Fenugreek) etc.

Sweets of Jharkhand

There is large variety of sweet delicacies available in tribal area due to cultural mix with their close neighbors from Bihar. Unlike Oriya and Bengali sweets, which are soaked in syrups made of sugar and are therefore wet, sweets of Tribal are mostly dry like Motichoor ka Ladoo, Khaja - This may be compared to the Greek baklava. Famous one is from Silao Nalanda, Tilkut (Til Burfi) - This is made of sesame seed and is available only in winters. A thick hard base of sugar of the size of a tennis ball is rolled in copious amount of sesame seed and then hammered to roll out in round shape. The more the seed, the softer, better and amorphous it is. Though available all over the state, the one from Gaya is famous. Malpua, Rabri/ Basundi, Kheer - A special form of kheer called Rasia is prepared during the Chhath festival, Thekua is very common preparation from wheat floor., Khajur, Laktho, Churma, Balushahi, Anarasa, Gulab Jamun. Kala Jamun, Pantua - Same as Kala Jamun but the shape is elongated. Famous one is from Kudu. Also called "Atom Bomb". Peda- Famous one is from Kesaria, khurma - found only in southwest of Bihar. Parwal ki Mithai - It is made of pointed gourd (botanical name-Trichosanthes dioica). The fruit is scrapped to remove the skin, sliced longitudinally, deseeded and boiled to make it tender and then filled with Khoyya- a preparation made of condensed milk and dry fruits. It is then imbibed with warm sugar syrup. Silver foil may be added after it cools off. Khubi ka Lai, Belgrami, Padokkia Pirikya - Made from flour and khoya etc. Kasar - A dry sweet prepared of coarsely ground rice during the Chhath festival. Gaja - It is a sweet which is cubical in form and made out of Maida.

Historical perspective or change over time is also crucial to understand a society's food culture. Another important premise is that the nature of food and food ways- even the best categories of what foods are "edible-are culturally defines and given local meanings, particularly as staple foods are placed at the centre of Culture and by taboos forbidding other items. More over, these staples play important role beyond the function of filling the stomach; by sustaining life they also sustain the self. For example, The Jharkhand tribes relish a beverage called "*Handia*" which is prepared by fermenting rice with the help of biro (a medicinal cake), partially cooked over fire in a *Handi* (earthen cooking pot). Then it is cooked and mixed with powdered biro. Then the pot is kept in a cool place for some days and after a certain time the "*Handia*" gets ready to be distributed. At any auspicious occasion, "*Handia*" (rice bear) which is said to be highly refreshing and invigorating and has great importance in their religious rites, is offered to deity, kinsmen and guests as a drink of honor.

To conclude, as a basic element of material culture and social life, food is the cultural trait that can be taken as cultural identity of Jharkhand which distinguishes it from other states.

References

Farb, Peter & Armelagos, G. 1998 *Consuming Passions: The Anthropology of Eating*. Boston: HoughtonMifflinBloomington, in: Indiana University Press.

http://journeymart.com/de/india/jharkhand/food.aspx

Haviland, W.A. 1981 Cultural Anthropology, Holt,Rinehart and Wilson, USA.

Kurlansky, M. 2007 "The Food Chains That Link Us All," *Time[Canadian Edition]*, July 30 – August 6, 41-43.

Enaaji, Moha. 2005 Multilingualism, Cultural Traits, and education in Morocco.

Tierney. R.K, and E.O Tierney 2012 Anthropology of food in J.P. Pilcher edited book Oxford Book of Food History, social science, Oxford University Press.

Chapter – 4

Political and Economic Movements in Jharkhand

What is a movement?

Movement means a group of people working together to advance their shared political, social, or artistic ideas." the labour movement".

In the social sciences, a political movement is a social group that operates together to obtain a political goal on a local, regional, national, or international scope. Political movements develop, coordinate, promulgate, revise, amend, interpret, and produce materials that are intended to address the goals of the base of the movement.

Some political movements have aimed to change government policy, such as the anti-war movement, the Ecology movement, and the Anti-globalization movement. Many have aimed to establish or broaden the rights of subordinate groups, such as abolitionism, the women's suffrage movement, the Civil rights movement, feminism, men's rights movement, etc.

In Jharkhand, a movement called "Naxalism" led by Left wing thinkers and activists seem to be the only major political movement after creation of Jharkhand.

In the recent years, Globalisation may be treated as economic movement – If we consider this, and then to the best of my knowledge-Microfinance movement through SHG can be placed in this category. Sustainable Development can be considered as another one in the list of economic movements in Jharkhand. I would like to share my thoughts in the above frame work.

Jharkhand case

Jharkhand is the second largest state inhabited by Tribal in India. They constitute nearly 26.7% of the population. Majority of tribal women do not undertake entrepreneurial ventures. Entrepreneurship is a key to economic development of a country.

Rapid growth of women's self-employment through SHGs and entrepreneurship confirms that this is an important avenue to improve women's employability. Fostering women's self-employment and entrepreneurship was also acknowledged as a policy priority by the regional Beijing + 5 meeting 2000.

Political movement-The Naxalites, Naxals or Naxal- wadis are a Maoist communist group in India, leaders of the Naxalite-Maoist insurgency. The Naxal name comes from the village of Naxalbari in the Indian state of West Bengal where the movement originated. The Naxals are considered far-left radical communists, supportive of Maoist political sentiment and ideology. Their origin can be traced to the split in 1967 of the Communist Party of India (Marxist), leading to the formation of the Communist Party of India (Marxist–Leninist). Initially the movement had its centre in West Bengal. In later years, it spread into less developed areas of rural central and eastern India, such as Chhattisgarh, Orissa and Andhra Pradesh through the activities of underground groups like the Communist Party of India (Maoist).[1]

As of 2009, Naxalites were active across approximately 220 districts in twenty states of India[2] accounting for about 40 percent of India's geographical area,[3] They are especially concentrated in an area known as the "Red Corridor", where they control 92,000 square kilometers.[3] According to India's intelligence agency, the Research and Analysis Wing, 20,000 armed cadre Naxalites were operating in addition to 50,000 regular cadres[4] and their growing influence prompted Indian Prime Minister Manmohan Singh to declare them to be the most serious internal threat to India's national security.[5]

The Naxalites are opposed by virtually all other Indian political groups.[6] In February 2009, the Indian Central government announced its plans for broad, co-ordinated operations in all affected states (Chhattisgarh, Orissa, Andhra Pradesh, Maharashtra, Jharkhand, Bihar, Uttar Pradesh, and West Bengal), to plug all possible escape routes of Naxalites.[7]

According to **Gyandeep Kaushal**, (12 Jun 2010) They make more destruction in Jharkhand when compared to states like Chattisgarh, West

Bengal, Maharastra, Uttar Pradesh, etc. The intensity of naxalism is highest in Jharkhand.

1. **Intensity of naxalism** - The naxalites are most active in Jharkhand.
2. **Almost fully infected** - Jharkhand seems to have been fully infected with this virus called naxalism. Leaving one district, namely, Sahibganj, all the other districts are affected by naxalites. The other states like other infected states like Orissa, Maharashtra etc. are not so badly infected.
3. **Naxal clamp downs** - In Jharkhand, the naxalites announce clamp downs the most. When compared to other states which are affected by naxalites, Jharkhand faces far more number of clamp downs (naxali bandi). Almost, in every two months, there is a naxal clamp down in Jharkhand.
4. **Tough to infiltrate** - Compared to other states like Maharashtra and Uttar Pradesh, Jharkhand is a plateau and the relief features here don't allow the armed authorities to penetrate deep into jungles, infiltrate it and fight naxals. Whenever, they tried to do so, most of the times, they lost their lives. Also, naxalism creates a deep effect on the economy of Jharkhand too, in the following ways –
    1. **Loss of Infrastructure** - Naxalites destroy raillines, important buildings like schools and hospital and cause a deep smash up to the infrastructural condition, which is already bad compared to other states.
    2. **Loss of lives** - Naxalites feel free to kill anyone, kidnap anyone to get their demands fulfilled. This has generated a very big threat to the lives of people of Jharkhand.
    3. **Social discrepancy** - Seeing what is happening, many youths in Jharkhand think that joining the naxalites is the only way to fight extreme poverty. Naxalism hits hard on the attitude of extremely poor people to work hard and earn.
    4. **Political instability** - Naxalism is a big cause to the frequent reallocations of Chief Ministers in Jharkhand. Whenever there is a hit by naxalites, the opposition criticizes the ruling party, and it plays a great role in removing them from chair. Though there may be other reasons too, but naxalism is definitely one of the biggest causes. (India study chanel.com)

Jharkhand: Naxal attacks kill 20 policemen in three days: Friday, June 12, 2009

Two days after they set off a landmine killing 10 policemen in West Singhbhum district, the CPI (Maoist) cadres on Friday launched synchronised attacks in Jharkhand, killing 10 policemen and leaving nine others wounded.

In a separate incident, a BJP leader, G Prasad, was shot dead by unidentified men at Belkuba Bazaar near the Jharkhand-Orissa border in Simdega district afternoon. Prasad, who owned a PDS shop, was attacked by three men on a motorcycle. The Maoists blew up an anti-landmine vehicle at Sarubeda between Nawadih and Bermo in Bokaro, over 150 km from Ranchi, killing eight Special Auxiliary Force personnel and wounding five other policemen and an eight-year-old girl. In Phusro in Bokaro district, over 100 armed Maoists, many of them women, attempted to loot a branch of the State Bank of India around 2 pm. But two policemen deployed there foiled the bid. "They resisted and did not let them get inside the bank," said Ranji Kumar, an SBI staffer. "Before fleeing, the Maoists overpowered both policemen, took their rifles and stabbed them to death." The policemen killed in the landmine blast were headed for the same SBI branch. "As part of reinforcement, the forces were going to the same SBI branch in an anti-landmine vehicle.The moment they drove over a culvert, the Maoists triggered the blast, killing the policemen and destroying the vehicle," said SP Laxman Prasad. (Manoj Prasad Posted: Saturday, Jun 13, 2009 at 0140 hrs IST, Ranchi)

The Naxalites blew up two school buildings in Banbirwa and Kone villages in Latehar district on Monday night. The two schools were kept reserve for the security forces as make-shift camps during the Assembly elections. One official in the state intelligence department said that Naxals had strengthen their activities in 18 Naxal-infested districts and sending messages to villagers not to cast their votes in the elections. The Union Home Ministry has decided to send 40 companies of Central Industrial Security Forces (CISF) to Jharkhand for holding free and fair polls.

Bokaro and Patna police in their joint operation on Tuesday at a co-operative colony in Bokaro, recovered one AK-47 rifle, two INSAS rifles, three hand grenades and nearly 32,000 cartridges of 12 bore, 22 guns and Naxal literature. In a related incident, responding to an order of the Jharkhand High Court dated September 16 on a public interest litigation filed by the People's Union of Civil Liberties (PUCL), the state government vacated 28 of the 43 schools which it had occupied for the use of security forces.It might be noted that Naxalism in Jharkhand came back under scanner again in the aftermath of the recent beheading of a police officer that grabbed national headlines.After the incident, the Centre has vowed to launch an operation against the Naxalites after the Jharkhand assembly polls. (Tapan Chakravorti / Kolkata/ Ranchi November 13, 2009, 0:15 IST referred in Business standard, September 2, 2010.)

Hazaribagh: The security forces on Friday exchanged gunfire in an encounter with the Naxalites, suspected to be of the Jharkhand Prastuti Committee, in the forests of Hazaribagh district, policesaid. "Bloodstains were found at the encounter site and the villagers claim to have seen two Naxalites, either injured or killed, being carried off by their associates," district Superintendent of Police Pankaj Kamboj told a agency. Apparently running out of ammunition and bullets, the Naxalites retreated deeper into the forests of Pandanwa, about 60 km from here, after trading gunfire for three hours, he added. Getting a tip-off that the ultras had gathered in the jungles, apparently to extort money from the contractors, a police task force, assisted by the India Reserve Battalion, reached the forests, Kamboj said. On seeing the security men, the naxalites fired, he said adding the strong reply by the security forces forced them to escape into the dense forests. The police recovered JPC-embossed uniform, utensils, a cell phone and literature, the police officer said. JPC is a breakaway group of the CPI (Maoist), he said. (Source: PTI Friday, April 02, 2010, 20:20)

Analysis

The above cases and many more, clearly indicate the deviant behaviors of the *pro people political outfit* in Jharkhand. If we look into the socio-economic condition that generated frustration among the poverty- ridden unemployed youth (male/female) then it will be clear that unemployment and poverty are twins that help in multiplying growth of insurgent situation leading to unrest.

Economic Movement-There is a need for development interventions to guide them on the path of progress. They need to be exposed to possibilities of innovation, targeting newer markets, establishing more linkages with distributors and suppliers and dealing with questions of product enhancement and diversification. Since this group has the potential of progressing more, mechanisms to promote their ambition is the need. SHGs can play major role in development process that may lead to peace and prosperity of Jharkhand.[8]

The issue of women's access to finance, and some of the challenges that women face in accessing finance are as follows:

- Women often have smaller amounts of personal capital available for start up

- Women have a greater need for external funding, yet have difficulty obtaining such funding
- Women lack knowledge about the available options, and the costs of getting this information (measured in money, time, energy) may be high due to family responsibilities
- Women may face explicit or implicit (structural) gender discrimination
- Banks may have inaccurate perceptions of women's borrowing and entrepreneurial behaviour.
- Banks often rely on personal profiles and track records in reviewing loan applications
- Women may be asked to pay a higher interest rate or provide higher guarantees

State government or NGOs should conduct researches and training programmes in following areas for preparing databases in their areas before and after introducing entrepreneurship packages.

- District Potential Studies
- Pre funding studies
- Specific Project Potential studies
- Documentation of project implementation
- Monitoring & Evaluation of SHG and Micro enterprise Project
- Evaluation studies of PMRY/SGSY/DUDA and others Development Project
- Specific Project impact studies
- Entrepreneurship Awareness Camps for creation of new enterprise
- Entrepreneurship Development Programme
- Product specific Programme
- Management development Programme
- Performance improvement Programme
- Export and marketing Programme
- Growth Programme for SME's
- Skill and Technology up gradation Programme etc.
- SHG and Micro enterprise Programme
- Trainer Training Programme

Following above strategy, Tribal women can be easily organized and trained in entrepreneurship as working in the field for economic increase, is inbuilt in their social system. Despite concerted efforts of governments and NGOs there are certain gaps. Of course we have come a long way in empowering women yet the future journey is difficult and demanding. In the light of facts enumerated in this paper, it is suggested that several programmes be initiated by the state authorities on the above lines for immediate and better results for promotion of Entrepreneurship especially among tribal women of Jharkhand.

Suggestions for promotion of Gender Entrepreneurship in Tribal and Rural Areas

To promote the tribal entrepreneurship in Jharkhand, a range of strategies can be used to address these challenges, such as:

- Special credit funds for tribal and rural women entrepreneurs.
- Mentoring or advisory services for tribal and rural women entrepreneurs.
- Development of ties with public authorities, business community, and networks.
- Flexible time schedules.
- Evaluation of loan applications based on business potential rather
- Strategies to change women entrepreneurs' self perceptions
- Strategies to promote a positive image of women entrepreneurs
- Various actors can play a role in facilitating women's access to finance, such as

  NABARD, CAPART, Nationalized Banks, Micro credit institutions, Private Banks, NGOs and Co-operatives.

Analysis

The processes of globalization are to be made on the theme- 'Think globally and act locally'. So at the local level the civil societies are to be formed into self-help groups at the village levels and subsequent federations from block to the divisions or districts for the entrepreneurial activities and for the community empowerment. Micro-finance has to be developed to develop small and micro-enterprise development. The human capital development in the tribal areas is to be strengthened by giving quality education or knowledge management in the SHG sector and also professional management system.[9]

A tailor made plan cannot be experimented everywhere, it should be area specific and demand based. If not, then, serious problems will arise.

Each & every area has different characteristics like language, natural resources, socio-economic & cultural conditions, human resources etc. For preparation of any developmental module, we cannot think in advance. It should be based on actual studies. For example, if anybody wants to introduce education in rural areas, it must be supported by appropriate Teaching & Learning Materials (TLM), sports, cultural activities etc., so that children can get attracted towards education. It has been felt that the children should be given value added education to make them good citizens.

References

1. Ramakrishnan, Venkitesh (2005-09-21). "The Naxalite Challenge". Frontline Magazine (The Hindu). http://www.flonnet.com/fl2221/stories/20051021006700400.htm. Retrieved 2007-03-15.
2. Handoo, Ashook. "Naxal Problem needs a holistic approach". Press Information Bureau. http://www.pib.nic.in/release/release.asp?relid=50833. Retrieved 2009-08-08.
3. 3."Rising Maoists Insurgency in India". Global Politician. 2007-01-15. http://globalpolitician.com/22790-india. Retrieved 2009-03-17.
4. Philip Bowring Published: TUESDAY, APRIL 18, 2006 (2006-04-18). "Maoists who menace India". International Herald Tribune. http://www.iht.com/articles/2006/04/17/opinion/edbowring.php. Retrieved 2009-03-17.
5. "South Asia | Senior Maoist 'arrested' in India". BBC News. 2007-12-19. http://news.bbc.co.uk/2/hi/south_asia/7151552.stm. Retrieved 2009-03-17.
6. Diwanji, A. K. (2003-10-02). "Primer: Who are the Naxalites?". Rediff.com. http://us.rediff.com/news/2003/oct/02spec.htm. Retrieved 2007-03-15.
7. Co-ordinated operations to flush out Naxalites soon The Economic Times, February 6, 2009.
8. Sharma. Vijay Prakash, Empowerment of Tribal Women: Issues and Challenges in Jharkhand, National Seminar on Issues and Challenges in Tribal Areas, University of Hyderabad, 29-30 March 2012.
9. Sharma. Vijay Prakash, Terrorism and Unemployment in India- a case from Jharkhand, UGC National Seminar, Rourkela, India. 29-30 Oct. 2010.

Chapter - 5

Environmental Stress and Displacement

Environmental issues are two fold in nature- (1) The limit to the natural resources and (2) pollution and stress that result from the exploitation of these resources. Displacement comes under the 2nd one. Let us examine some cases of displacement in our countryand Its Consequences.

Case 1 - The Issue of Mega Dam

It is now over six decades that the Koel- Karo Hydro-electric project and Swarnrekha multipurpose projects are hanging in air and has become stagnant. Even the employees of the projects think that the cloud of uncertainty looms large over the entire project. Koel- Karo Hydro-electric project in Bihar(now in Jharkhand) was initially started an envisaged by the Bihar State Electricity Board in consultation with the earstwhile central water and power commission between 1959-1973. It was I the year 1981 that the entire charge of its construction and power distribution was handed over to NHEPC. Delay in its construction is not only causing huge national loss. The more the delay the more the cost of its installation that comes from tax-payers money. In the meantime, thc displaced families spent all the money received as compensation and are now paupers. This displacement created a new kind of cultural stress that resulted into strong resentment and resistance from the people, particularly the tribals on cultural and religious grounds against the project. They were in no mood to shift their SARNAS and SASANDIRIS from its original place to another. They were of opinion that, "government can rehabilitate us physically, but will uproot us culturally." 106 villages with 8423 land owners were affected/uprooted and displaced under this project.

Now let us move from Jharkhand to an interpretation of the ongoing debates in the politics of Assam regarding the probable consequences of Mega dam project in Arunachal Pradesh. Big Dams in India, whether it is Polavaram dam in Andhra Pradesh, Mullaperiyar dam in Kerala, Tehri dam in Uttaranchal, Narmada Dams in Gujarat and Madhya pradesh or Medium and Major Dams for Hydro-power in Arunachal pradesh, Nepaland in other parts of Himalayan Mountains, proper Environmental Impact Analysis Reports, Disaster Management, Risk and Dam-Break Analysis, Environmental management plans are prepared and placed before the public as per rules and regulations and the Union ministries are simplifying condoning these grave mistakes which compromise with the future of the nation at very great cost. It is reflected in the scenario of big HE projects which will be built in Arunachal Pradesh at the cost of lives of millions of residents in the downstream of river Subanshiri. These short of big dams will destroy agricultural land & biodiversity of the region. Interest of central govt. is to provide enormous power to northern India. To fulfill the power requirement in north India it can sacrifice northeast India. Unfortunately this is the center's policy since independence. Assam Dams are going to burst and cause economic losses worth several lakhs of cores of rupees to the Indian nation besides killing lakhs of people of Assam, located on the margins of Brahmaputra River and its several tributaries. It is argued that intellectuals are miserably failing in creating awareness on these large constructions of dams in Assam region where major earth quakes are waiting in the wings and these Major dams become man-made disasters. We need not blame China for tapping Brahmaputra water by dams for power generation in the Tibet region as we are planning more disasters in the form of Hydro-power plants in Arunachal pradesh which is under the influence of the rich contractors who hail from outside the North Eastern states.

Case 2 - Development Projects and Displacement

The case study is an attempt to assess the impact of development projects on socio-cultural and economic life of tribal of Gabaraghathy Birsa-Munda Rehabilitation colony of Kalinga Nagar, Jajpur district of Odisha.

Developments refer to the change in quality of life towards betterment, to growth, progress, improvement and expansion of a complex process involving the social, cultural, political and economic betterment of people and of society. Government of India has been implementing many development projects in the tribal areas and they were literally chased away from their own traditional land and turned into displaced, land less, migrant people in search of a livelihood. The rehabilitation and resettlement policy of the governments is yet to be successful and women are suffering both by state machineries and customary practices. The present setting of tribal livelihood is changing from its traditional root due to the growth of urbanization, industrialization cash economy etc. which are promoted by the state with the influence of economic liberalization- privatization-globalization which is called as LPG model. In the name of developing the backward regions, the present model of development is focuses on such as industry, mining, hydropower projects, big dams, etc. in the natural resources regions. These projects require huge land acquisition, deforestation and depletion natural resources for their establishment. As a result, livelihood of the tribal in now under threat because they are becoming the victims of land alienation, poverty and bonded labour. Generally, dispute associated with these tribal communities are less support, insufficient compensation, loss of livelihood, increase in stress and health problem as well as loss of their identities.

Case 3 - A Critical Studies of Tribal Rights *vs.* Environmental Conservation under FRA, 2006

The governance and utilization of India's forests are judged by two major politicized state laws; ***Indian Forest Act, 1927*** and the ***Wild Life (Protection) Act, 1972,*** which empowers the government to declare any area to be a reserved forest, protected forest, village forest, protected area, national park, wildlife sanctuary, tiger reserve or community conservation area. Contrary to these laws, the recently passed Scheduled Tribes and Other Traditional Forest Dwellers (Recognition of Forest Rights) Act, 2006, justifies the rights of forest-dwelling communities to land and other resources, denied to them over decades as a result of the continuance of colonial forest laws in India. On this background, we need to critically examine the compatibility of state laws and the tribal's rights. Firstly, to know the historicity of the 'depth of injustice' and how the rights were to be recognized? And Secondly, to see whether the forest rights threaten wildlife conservation or not. Thirdly, critically look at the politics; intention, structure and impact related arguments behind making of this Act. Harmonization of customary laws and the politicized statutory laws for protection of tribal rights and conservation of the forest.

Case 4 - Development Induced Displacement

There is evidence of development-induced displacement which continues from the pre-independence era. Every day the development projects are affecting numerous peoples and communities across the globe. The model of development is broadly understood in terms of the technological and industrial interventions for "modernizing" society'. Though they bring economic prosperity but at the same time they create an unpleasant and undesirable displacement of section of population from their ancestral habitat, uprooting them from their immovable properties, their live stock, wealth, religious and educational institutions etc. Installing major hydropower dams, irrigation and drinking water systems, industrial projects, extending highways and other infrastructural projects such as hotels, resorts, airports, ports, towns, sewage system, transmission lines, subways, intra-city roads, etc in the name of development resulted into hardship and deprivation. These development projects have been displacing inhabitants involuntarily and out of these ousters most of the peoples are underprivileged and backward sections living in the remote areas of the society. Around one million peoples displaced every year since independence says a report released recently by a working group on Human rights in India and the United Nations. Of these displaced over 40% are tribal's and another 40% are lower caste and rural poor. It alienates these people from their traditional sources of subsistence, such as lands, forest and village habitats and gives rise to severe social, economic, psychological problems. They are bound to live in a new atmosphere in a new place with new attitude and values. Their hearth, livelihood, social capital, culture, basic social structure everything are greatly jeopardized by these projects and resulted in to severe long-term hardship, impoverishment and environmental damage and the affected person reaches a stage of hand to mouth existence. The rustic nature of the legal provisions' regarding the land acquisition, displacement and rehabilitation and its exploitative temperament in India enhances the plight of poor and downtrodden. Their entire problems are always dealt with an ad-hoc and haphazard manner. Despite their a great sacrifice for the enrichment of the country no one hear their problem empathetically so they lead a miserable life by losing everything. Now-a-days this is a very sensitive issue so it should be studied and their problems need to be addressed at the policy level.

Case 5 - the Unresolved Issues of Displacement Induced Development

The dichotomous issues of displacement and development have been a seminal concern in the development paradigm of India since independence. In spite of many attempts to define and redefine the concept of development by the academia to civil society organizations, there is no such definition of development which can be acceptable to all sections of the society. Though passing of the Rehabilitation and resettlement Policy and many amendments brought to it has improved the situation, it has yet many unresolved issues. Against this backdrop, the present case is an attempt to analyze a case of displacement related problems in Basantpur Gram Panchayat of Sambalpur district. Relevant data have been collected through government records and files, personal interview, formal meetings and focused group discussion. The mauza Basantpur is one of the six mauzas that were acquired by the state government for the purpose of one proposed Chipilma subsidiary reservoir in the year 1946. The plan for building the subsidiary reservoir was abandoned in the year 1952 and instead of the reservoir the existing Chipilma Power Channel was constructed. Out of the 7500 acres of land acquired by the government for the only 500 acres was utilized for the construction of the power channel. According to land acquisition manual Bihar and Odisha Act-1929, the surplus land of 7000 acres acquired for the Chipilma reservoir should have been relinquished by the government and ought to have been redistributed among the villagers of the acquired villages. But the state government failed to abide by the prevailing law and did not relinquished the surplus land but continued to give yearly lease of the land for the purpose of cultivation to the villagers concerned on payment of nominal land till 1990.

From the year 1991, the government again started taking tax and filed encroachment against the farmers instead of giving on land lease as per the previous practice. The same trend continues till date. The government has started different projects like Agriculture farm, Fishery Farm, Central Cattle Breeding Firm from time to time in the same land. Presently the government has planned to establish Sainik School, Reserve Police Campus and forcefully acquiring land from the villagers which they have been cultivating. The people are not interested to leave the land but the government claims that the land has already been acquired. The government is also not interested to pay any compensation to the people as the compensation has already been given to the people with a rate of 50-100 per acre depending upon the land type during that time. Since the people of the study area do not possess *Patta,* they are deprived of many of the government schemes and subsidies. It is found during the study that the people are in constant fear and anxiety due to the loss of land.

Case 6 - Mega Development: economic marginalization of artisans' communities

The artisans' communities and their traditional knowledge on handicrafts in the sample area have been experiencing a great threat for live, livelihood and loss of knowledge. The production of handicrafts is a skill which passes down from one generation to successive generation orally. The establishments of mega development projects in this region have not only impacted the live and livelihood of agricultural communities but threaten the artisan' communities also in a great extent. Many of them have lost the sources of livelihood indirectly due to the acquisition of land. All handmade crafts have a socio-cultural and economic value related with land. Traditionally all agricultural implements, household articles and need of goods related to various socio-cultural practices were provided by the concerned artisan community to the villagers. Among them were basket weaver, carpenter, blacksmith and potter. In the present scenario many of them are jobless with hardly any scope for economic opportunities except marginal labour work under the contractors. Their situations far more are worse than the people who directly related to land because they get nothing as compensation as they are landless. Information is collected from the effected villages of Vedanta Aluminum & Power, Bhusan Steel & Power and Hindal Co.

Discussion

People who are forced to flee from a disaster or conflict usually receive sympathetic attention and international aid. The same cannot be said for the millions of people worldwide who have been displaced by development, even though the consequences they face may be comparably dire. Here as per the corollary of aforementioned statement, development is necessary but that shouldn't infringe the basic right of other people.

In decades past, the dominant view of the third world societies who were involved in the "development" was that they should transformed the traditional and simple structure into modern, complex, Westernized countries. Seen in this light, large-scale, capital-intensive development projects accelerated the pace toward a brighter and better future. If, in the name of development people were uprooted, then either they will suffer or as per the change in circumstances it may be beneficial for them.

In recent decades, however, a new development paradigm has been articulated, one that promotes poverty reduction, environmental protection, social justice, and human rights. In this paradigm, development is seen as both bringing benefits and imposing costs. In greatest costs it includes displacement of millions of vulnerable people due to construction of dams, roads, ports, railways and exploration of mines. In all cases displacement raises important ethical questions. What is owed to people who are displaced? Under what conditions can development that includes displacement are justified? What kind of ethical analysis can provide justification for displacement-inducing development?

Conclusion- Environmental issues are two fold in nature- (1) The limit to the natural resources and (2) pollution and stress that result from the exploitation of these resources

Ecological control is necessary that deals with both the above mentioned aspects i.e. (1) by changing the mix of these resources in favour of renewable resources and (2) by inducing an improvement in resource productivity. For these purposes, it would be necessary to deploy a combination of measures, viz, investment, research for development of environment friendly technologies, economic incentives and disincentives. However, there needs to be a difference in the approach to the problem in the developing countries (including ours) from that in the developed countries. The environmental standards cannot be the same for these two sets of economies. The immediate environmental concerns and issues in developing country like India are- land degradation, soil erosion, disaster management, over chemicalisation of crop production, air and water pollution including ground water pollution, recycling of waste, increasing pressures on life supporting systems, and socio-economic impact of development projects including human displacement and loss of bio diversity.

Sectoral plans are a way forward. A tailor made plan cannot be experimented everywhere, it should be area specific and demand based. If not, then, serious problems will arise. Each & every area has different characteristics like language, natural resources, socio-economic &cultural conditions, human resources etc. For preparation of any developmental module, we cannot think in advance. It should be based on actual studies. For example, if anybody wants to introduce education in rural areas, it must be supported by appropriate Teaching & Learning Materials (TLM), sports, cultural activities etc., so that children can get attracted towards education. It has been felt that the children should be given value added education to make them good citizens.

Two very important ethical issues suggested by Anil Agrawal may be kept in mind-

1. Environmental destruction is largely caused by the consumption of the rich.
2. The worst sufferers of environmental destruction are poor.

The government cannot escape the charge of creating more complexities than addressing the issue that is helping in disguise the left wing extremism to prosper.

I would like to conclude, with the following lines of ~ **Mohandas Karamchand Gandhi.**

"Earth Provides Enough To Satisfy Every Man's Need But Not Every Man's Greed."

References

1. The Issue of Mega Dam and Its Probable Consequences on the Marginalized Communities of Assam,*Dr. Bikash Deka,Assistant Professor, Department of Sociology, Dibrugarh University, Assam, Email- bikash.dk01@gmail.com*
2. Development Projects and Displacement: Impact on Tribal of Kalinga Nagar, Odisha, India: An Anthropological perspective, *Biswajit Parida, Research Scholar, Department of Anthropology, Sambalpur University, Jyoti Vihar, Odisha, Email: parida.biswa85@gmail.com*
3. Beyon Politicised Law: A Critical Study of Tribal Rights *vs.* Environmental Conservation under FRA, 2006 ,*Dr.Debendra Kumar Biswal, Assistant Professor, Centre for Tribal and Customary Law ,Central University of Jharkhand, Brambe, Ranchi, Jharkhand, PIN-764020*
4. +91-9973579387 (M), EmalI: debendra.biswal@cuj.ac.in
5. Development Induced Displacement: A Bane for the Underprivileged Communities in India, *Jayadev Satapathy, Research Schoolar, Central University Of Odisha, Koraput*
6. E-Mail- satapathy.jayadev6@gmail.com
7. The Unresolved Issues of Displacement Induced Development: A Case Analysis from a Small Town of Western Odisha, *Madan Biswal, Faculty MSW Course, Sambalpur University*
8. Rakesh Kumar Padhan,Manager (Adm), Vision India Foundation Sambalpur
9. Mega Development: A Threat to Live and Livelihood of Artisan' Community, *Minaketan Bag,Research Scholar,Department of Anthropology, Sambalpur University, E-mail: bag.minaanth@gmail.com*
10. Socio Legal Aspect of Dilemmas of Development Induced Displacement, *Rajesh Kumar Mishra, Author, LL.M. student from Hidayatullah National Law University, Raipur, Chhattisgarh, Nidhi Jaiswal,Co-Author, LL.M. student from Hidayatullah National Law University, Raipur, Chhattisgarh.*
11. Ecology and sustainable development, R. Thamarajlaxmi review of book, Ecological Economics: A practical Programme for Global Reform, the group of green economists, Zed books, London, 1992 in Economic and political weekly, April 24, 1993.

Chapter – 6

Gender and Livelihood: Needed Women Entrepreneurship in Jharkhand

Jharkhand is the second largest state inhabited by Tribal in India. They constitute nearly 26.7% of the population. Majority of tribal women do not undertake entrepreneurial ventures. Entrepreneurship is a key to economic development of a country.

Rapid growth of women's self-employment through SHGs and entrepreneurship confirms that this is an important avenue to improve women's employability. Fostering women's self-employment and entrepreneurship was also acknowledged as a policy priority by the regional Beijing +5 meeting 2000.

Majority of tribal women do not undertake entrepreneurial ventures. Entrepreneurship is a key to economic development of a country. The government programme for women development began as early as 1954 in India but the actual participation began only in 1974. At present, the Government of India has over 27 schemes for women operated by different departments and ministries. The schemes for training and skill development, and provision for credit, infrastructure, marketing which are critical to women's economic independence and autonomy has very little share.

A general lack of consistent data and research on self-employment, and in particular gender disaggregated data, means that we know little about women's entrepreneurship. Although women face common challenges related to starting and building up their businesses, their experiences vary.

Women want better access to education, training, and counseling. Access to capital is a very important issue for many women business owners, who often lack formal education in financial matters and who may face gender-based barriers to accessing financing. Women want full access to business networks such as industry-specific and general business associations.Women want to be treated seriously as business owners.

Methods

This paper examines the problems of Gender Livelihood in Jharkhand and Constraints of SHG promotion in most tribal dominated backward regions. The primary data collected from Left wing extremist area of Chaibasa, palamu and Ranchi district and secondary data collected from Jharkhand government socio- economic survey report 2014, internet files and libraries.

Discussion

Many tribal women business owners, often lack formal education in financial matters face gender-based barriers to accessing financing. In Jharkhand, one finds a sub-group of tribal women who are last also in terms of development and expansion potential. They are satisfied with their limited growth. The growth of their enterprises is stagnant mainly because they have consciously chosen to continue to operate at this particular level. This can be partly attributed to limited ambition and partly to the convenience they see in operating like this: goods produced and sold informally, reasonable profit made, they're quite comfortable earning this way, so they knowingly choose not to struggle anymore

There is a need for development interventions to guide them on the path of progress. They need to be exposed to possibilities of innovation, targeting newer markets, establishing more linkages with distributors and suppliers and dealing with questions of product enhancement and diversification. Since this group has the potential of progressing more, mechanisms to promote their ambition is the need.

There are three major problems in Gender Livelihood promotion in Jharkhand (1) *Access to information* (2) Access *to capital and* (3) Access to *networks*.

In tribal area like Jharkhand, economic opportunities for women are scarce while hardships are plentiful. Women often see little hope for themselves or their children to improve their future.

It is suggested that local institutions should play a pro-active role to formulate norms and methods to tackle the problem of poverty in rural areas. Though the large number of women related legislations are in place, it is seen that the efficacy of these laws are not satisfactory primarily on account of poor implementation. A major reason for this is the lack of adequate knowledge and awareness regarding these special legislations. Also there is absence of gender sensitivity on part of the functionaries at the Panchayat levels such as law enforcement, police, prosecution, medical profession, education etc.

There is a need to give a very high priority to training and capacity building of among the Tribal women especially at Panchayat level. Women are regaining the sense of self-worth and are no longer willing to take a backseat. They want to be treated with respect and dignity and now hate any ideas or ideology that treat them as a commodity. They want to take decisions on matters bearing on them. Women want access to opportunities and resources, without any discrimination, for their economic independence. They want to be able to influence the social and other changes playing a more active role in nation building activities.

Last but not the least they want total control on their own lives without any undue interference from any quarter.

A substantial number of Scheduled Tribes (STs) women have been elected to the Panchayats.

Therefore, provisions of Social Justice Committee at different levels of Panchayats will have a reasonable positive effect towards their empowerment. It is also true that caste discrimination and atrocities on scheduled castes and Tribes households continue unabated in various states, this is so despite various constitutional provisions and legislative measures. Thus, elected women Panchayat representatives, particularly from ST communities face enormous discriminations in performing their public roles effectively. While continued discrimination in society has a very complex reality, what is really worrisome is that government officials also treat such elected Panchayat representatives with neglect and apathy. Such attitudes and practices further limit the effectiveness of elected Panchayat representatives from ST households. It is therefore, suggested that following action need to be taken up; Social Justice Committees should be legislated to be an integral part of each tier of the Panchayat Raj system in all states. Ministry of Panchayati Raj, Government of India, can target its BRGF grants to those Gram Panchayats and Panchayat Samitis, which are headed by ST elected representatives. The Ministries of Panchayati Raj and Rural Development, Government of India, can further utilize BRGF, NREGS, IAY and SGSY resources to undertake specially targeted capacity enhancement programmes for elected Panchayat leaders of women in general and ST women in particular. Civil society organizations should be mobilized to join in capacity building of the target population, which among other things could also include literacy skills like rapid reading.

State government or NGOs should conduct researches and training programmes in following areas for preparing databases in their areas before and after introducing gender livelihood and entrepreneurship packages.

1. District Potential Studies
2. Pre funding studies
3. Specific Project Potential studies
4. Documentation of project implementation
5. Monitoring & Evaluation of SHG and Micro enterprise Project
6. Evaluation studies of PMRY/SGSY/DUDA and others Development Project
7. Specific Project impact studies
8. Entrepreneurship Awareness Camps for creation of new enterprise
9. Entrepreneurship Development Programme
10. Product specific Programme
11. Management development Programme
12. Performance improvement Programme
13. Export and marketing Programme
14. Growth Programme for SME's
15. Skill and Technology up gradation Programme etc.
16. SHG and Micro enterprise Programme
17. Trainer Training Programme

Tribal women can be easily organized and trained in livelihood entrepreneurship as working in the field for economic increase is inbuilt in their social system.

Despite concerted efforts of governments and NGOs there are certain gaps. Of course we have come a long way in empowering women yet the future journey is difficult and demanding. In the light of facts enumerated in this paper, it is suggested that gender based livelihood programmes be initiated by the state authorities on the above lines for immediate and better results for promotion of Gender Livelihood especially among tribal women of Jharkhand.

To promote the gender livelihood entrepreneurship among tribal women of Jharkhand, a range of strategies can be used to address these challenges, such as:

1. Special credit funds for tribal and rural women entrepreneurs.
2. Mentoring or advisory services for tribal and rural women entrepreneurs
3. Development of ties with public authorities, business community, and networks
4. Flexible time schedules.
5. Evaluation of loan applications based on business potential rather than past track record
6. Strategies to change women entrepreneurs' self perceptions
7. Strategies to promote a positive image of women entrepreneurs
8. Various actors can play a role in facilitating women's access to finance,

Such as NABARD, CAPART, Nationalized Banks, Micro credit institutions, Private Banks, NGOs and Co-operatives .

Women empowerment and planning process in India

The all round development of women has been one of the focal point of planning process in India. The First Five-Year Plan (1951-56) envisaged a number of welfare measures for women. Establishment of the Central Social Welfare Board, organization of Mahila Mandals and the Community Development Programmes were a few steps in this direction.

In the second Five-Year Plan (1956-61), the empowerment of women was closely linked with the overall approach of intensive agricultural development programmes.

The Third and Fourth Five-Year Plans (1961-66 and 1969-74) supported female education as a major welfare measure.

The Fifth Five-Year Plan (1974-79) emphasized training of women, who were in need of income and protection. This plan coincided with International Women's Decade and the submission of Report of the Committee on the Status of Women in India. In 1976, Women's welfare and Development Bureau was set up under the Ministry of Social Welfare.

The Sixth Five-Year Plan (1980-85) saw a definite shift from welfare to development. It recognized women's lack of access to resources as a critical factor hindering their growth.

The Seventh Five-Year Plan (1985-90) emphasized the need for gender equality and empowerment. For the first time, emphasis was placed upon qualitative aspects such as inculcation of confidence, generation of awareness with regards, to rights and training in skills for better employment.

The Eight Five-Year Plan (1992-97) focused on empowering women, especially at the grass roots level, through Panchayati Raj Institutions.

The Ninth Five-Year Plan (1997-2002) adopted a strategy of women's component plan, under which not less than 30 percent of funds/benefits were earmarked for women-specific programmes.

The Tenth Five-Year Plan (2002-07) aims at empowering women through translating the recently adopted National Policy for Empowerment of Women (2001) into action and ensuring Survival, Protection and Development of women and children through rights based approach.

Gender Budgeting approach

In India, gender perspective on public expenditure had been gaining ground since the publication of the report of the Committee on the Status of Women in 1974. The Eighth Five Year Plan (1992-97) highlighted for the first time the need to ensure a definite flow of funds from the general developmental sectors to women. The Plan document made an express statement that "…the benefits of development from different sectors should not by pass women and special programmes on women should complement the general development programmes. The latter, in turn, should reflect greater gender sensitivity". This approach, however, could not make much dent in ensuring adequate flow of funds and benefits to women.

The gender budgeting initiative in India started in July 2000 when a Workshop on 'Engendering National Budgets in the South Asia Region' was held in New Delhi in collaboration with the UNIFEM, in which Government representatives, UN agencies, media, NGOs, research institutions, civil society and members of the Planning Commission in the South Asia region participated.

Gender Budgeting is not a separate budget for women; rather it is a dissection of the government budget to establish its gender-differential impacts and to translate gender commitments into budgetary commitments.

The main objective of a gender-sensitive budget is to improve the analysis of incidence of budgets, attain more effective targeting of public expenditure and offset any undesirable gender-specific consequences of previous budgetary measures.

An analysis of gender budget of government of India reveals that this budget takes into account the fund allocation more towards social services area than economic services. The schemes for training and skill development, and provision for credit, infrastructure, marketing which are critical to women's economic independence and autonomy has very little share.

A better allocation of budget share should be made under ministry of industries than social welfare and others.

Majority of women do not undertake entrepreneurial ventures. Entrepreneurship is a key to economic development of a country. Gender budgeting for women is a dissection of the government budget to establish its gender-differential impacts and to translate gender commitments into budgetary commitments but this is not enough. An analysis of gender budget of government of India reveals that this budget takes into account the fund allocation more towards social services area than economic services. The schemes for training and skill development, and provision for credit, infrastructure, marketing which are critical to women's economic independence and autonomy has very little share.

Most poor and low-income citizens in India are in the informal sector of the economy. How can development initiatives working with informal sector workers be successful?

A better allocation of budget share should be made under ministry of industries than social welfare and others.

Constraints of SHG promotion in most backward regions

Though the left wing is not against development but their activities presents them as villain to the common mass. In Jharkhand, Out of 24 districts, Naxalites have strong holds in 18 districts of Jharkhand. Now, the officials responsible for governing/protecting the State are forced to focus on the problems which are the outcomes of two factors-Poverty and unemployment. The officials should spend more time and money in solving these problems than promoting Green hunt mission if they really want to address the problem. Unfortunately, they are getting themselves far away from the root cause that will only lead to embarrassment. Sometimes, these officials also make use of this confused state to fulfill their pockets and this in turn adding fuel to the fire. The Naxalites, Naxals or Naxal- wadis are a Maoist communist group in India, leaders of the Naxalite-Maoist insurgency. The Naxal name comes from the village of Naxalbari in the Indian state of West Bengal where the movement originated. The Naxals are considered far-left radical communists, supportive of Maoist political sentiment and ideology. Their origin can be traced to the split in 1967 of the Communist Party of India (Marxist), leading to the formation of the Communist Party of India (Marxist–Leninist). Initially the movement had its centre in West Bengal. In later years, it spread into less developed areas of rural central and eastern India, such as Jharkhand, Chhattisgarh, Orissa and Andhra Pradesh through the activities of underground groups like the Communist Party of India (Maoist). This movement is badly affecting progress in rural areas of Jharkhand. Women don't feel secured and are hesitant to participate in government promoted programmes.

Conclusion

The schemes for training and skill development and provision for credit, infrastructure, marketing which are critical to women's economic independence and autonomy has been remained a neglected area that requires immediate attention for developing gender based entrepreneurship in India. Various development programmes have been implemented by the government to protect tribal women from social injustice and all forms of exploitation and to uplift their standard of living. Increasingly large amount is being spent, over the years, both by the Central and State govt. for the development of the Tribal area but the result is far from satisfaction level.

Tribal women need to be trained to play their active role in Panchayati Raj Institution and avail the benefits. There is a need to have capacity building Initiatives and training, orientation in Panchayati Raj Institutions (PRIs), Accountability & Transparency, Development of Model Gram Panchayats, Panchayat Extension of Scheduled Area Act (PESA) and Backward Regions Grant Fund should be ensure that its benefits reaches to the Gram Panchayat level and helps to strengthen gender livelihood among tribal communities.

A tailor made plan cannot be experimented everywhere, it should be area specific and demand based. If not, then, serious problems will arise. Each & every area has different characteristics like language, natural resources, socio-economic & cultural conditions, human resources etc. For preparation of any developmental module, we cannot think in advance. It should be based on actual studies.The processes of globalization are to be made on the theme- 'Think globally and act locally'. So at the local level the civil societies are to be formed into self-help groups at the village levels and subsequent federations from block to the divisions or districts for the entrepreneurial activities and for the community empowerment. Micro-finance has to be developed for gender livelihood promotion. The human capital development in the tribal areas is to be strengthened by giving quality education or knowledge management in the SHG sector and also professional management system.

References

Dasgupta. Tapati, et al. Gender Entrepreneurship in a Rural Scenario: A Case Study of South West Midnapore, West Bengal, J. Soc. Sci., 12(2): 151-158. 2006.

Ewa Ruminska-ZimnyMaking Self-Employment an Important Opportunity for Women, *UNECE.* 2003.

Ram Rajput et.al Gender Budget Initiative, Report of SSRO for Gender Budget, nd.

Sharma. Vijay Prakash,"Tribal Women Empowerment through PRI (Key Speech) UGC National seminar Tribal women in Panchayati Raj Institutions", Department of Sociology, Neelsaila Mahavidyalaya, Rourkela, Orissa10-11 November 2013.

——Participatory Development, Ramesh Chandra edited book Tribal Development and Administration and Management, DEC, National Institute of Rural Development, Ministry of Rural Development, Government of India, Hyderabad (AP), India, 2013.

——Empowerment of Tribal Women: Issues and Challenges in Jharkhand, National Seminar on Issues and Challenges in Tribal Areas, University of Hyderabad, 29-30 March 2012.

——Gender Entrepreneurship in Rural and Tribal Areas: Problems and Prospects, in P.K.Bhowmick et.al. Edited book Tribal Life and Gender Entrepreneurship, ISRAA, Bidisa, 2011.

——Health Empowerment of Women in Jharkhand, SOCIAL MODERNITY, Asian Journal of Social Science Vol. I, No. 1-2, Ranchi, India, June-Dec.2010

—— Terrorism and Unemployment in India- a case from Jharkhand, UGC National Seminar, Rourkela, India. 29-30 Oct. 2010.

——Report on Socio-Economic Survey of Palamau coal Mining Area and Development of Rehabilitation and Resettlement Plan, Kolkata, 2004.

——Report on Socio-Economic Survey of Iron Ore Mining Area (Saranda, West Singbhum) and planning social development, Kolkata, 2004.

Chapter - 7

Constraints of SHG promotion in most backward regions, Tribal dominated and left-wing influenced areas

Jharkhand is the second largest state inhabited by Tribal in India. They constitute nearly 26.7% of the population. Majority of tribal women do not undertake entrepreneurial ventures. Entrepreneurship is a key to economic development of a country.

Rapid growth of women's self-employment through SHGs and entrepreneurship confirms that this is an important avenue to improve women's employability. Fostering women's self-employment and entrepreneurship was also acknowledged as a policy priority by the regional Beijing +5 meeting 2000.

A general lack of consistent data and research on self-employment, and in particular gender disaggregated data, means that we know little about women's entrepreneurship. Although women face common challenges related to starting and building up their businesses, their experiences vary. Women want better access to education, training, and counseling. Access to capital is a very important issue for many women business owners, who often lack formal education in financial matters and who may face gender-based barriers to accessing financing. Women want full access to business networks such as industry-specific and general business associations. Women want to be treated seriously as business owners. This paper examines the problems of tribal women entrepreneurship in Jharkhand and Constraints of SHG promotion in most backward regions, tribal dominated and left-wing influenced areas to seek immediate intervention.

The issue of **women's access to finance**, and some of the challenges that women face in accessing finance are as follows: Women often have smaller amounts of personal capital available for start up. They have a greater need for external funding, yet have difficulty obtaining such funding. Women may face explicit or implicit (structural) gender discrimination and Banks may have inaccurate perceptions of women's borrowing and entrepreneurial behaviour.

Majority of women do not undertake entrepreneurial ventures. Entrepreneurship is a key to economic development of a country. Gender budgeting for women is a dissection of the government budget to establish its gender-differential impacts and to translate gender commitments into budgetary commitments but this is not enough. An analysis of gender budget of government of India reveals that this budget takes into account the fund allocation more towards social services area than economic services. The schemes for training and skill development, and provision for credit, infrastructure, marketing which are critical to women's economic independence and autonomy has very little share. The government programme for women development began as early as 1954 in India but the actual participation began only in 1974. At present, the Government of India has over 27 schemes for women operated by different departments and ministries. The schemes for training and skill development, and provision for credit, infrastructure, marketing which are critical to women's economic independence and autonomy has very little share.

Discussion

There are three major problems in Tribal women entrepreneurship in Jharkhand ***(1) Access to information (2)*** **Access** ***to capital and (3)*** **Access to** ***networks.***

Many tribal women business owners, often lack formal education in financial matters face gender-based barriers to accessing financing. In Jharkhand, one finds a sub-group of tribal women who are last also in terms of development and expansion potential. They are satisfied with their limited growth. The growth of their enterprises is stagnant mainly because they have consciously chosen to continue to operate at this particular level. This can be partly attributed to limited ambition and partly to the convenience they see in operating like this: goods produced and sold informally, reasonable profit made, they're quite comfortable earning this way, so they knowingly choose not to struggle anymore. Sixty percent of women have some money that they can decide how to use. The proportion of women with money which they control is highest for women in the highest wealth quintile and women with at least 10 years of education. Only 14 percent of women have a bank or savings account that they themselves use.

Women's knowledge and use of microcredit programmes is fairly limited. Only 26 percent of women have heard of any microcredit programme in the area and only 2 percent have ever used one.

Only 51 percent of women are allowed to go by themselves to the market, only 47 percent are allowed to go by themselves to a health facility, and only 40 percent are allowed to go by themselves to places outside their own village or community.

Overall, 37 percent of women are allowed to go alone to all three of these places. Older women, scheduled-tribe women, women in nuclear households, and those with 10 or more years of education have more freedom of movement than other women.

Tribal dominated and left-wing influenced areas - Constraints of SHG promotion in most backward regions-

Though the left wing is not against development but their terrorizing activities presents them as villain to the common mass. The fear psychosis created by them in tribal villages is badly affecting the SHG promotion in rural areas of Jharkhand . Out of 24 districts Naxalites have strong holds in 18 districts of Jharkhand. Now, the officials responsible for governing/ protecting the State are forced to focus on the problems which are the outcomes of two factors-Poverty and unemployment. The officials should spend more time and money in solving these problems than promoting Green hunt mission if they really want to address the problem. Unfortunately, they are getting themselves far away from the root cause that will only lead to embarrassment. Sometimes, these officials also make use of this confused state to fulfill their pockets and this in turn adding fuel to the fire.

A status paper on problems of left wing extremism presented to home ministry in 2006, indicated that" the Naxlites operate in the vacuum created by absence of administrative and political institutions support the local demands and take advantage of the disenchantment prevented among the exploited section of the population and seek to offer an alternative system of governance. There is a need to create confidence among SHG groups that their livelihood supporting activities will not be allowed to hamper by the Naxals.

A general lack of consistent data and research on self-employment, and in particular gender disaggregated data, means that we know little about women's entrepreneurship. Although women face common challenges related to starting and building up their businesses, their experiences vary. Women want better access to education, training, and counseling. Access to capital is a very important issue for many women business owners, who often lack formal education in financial matters and who may face gender-based barriers to accessing financing. Women want full access to business networks such as industry-specific and general business associations. Women want to be treated seriously as business owners. This paper examines the problems of tribal women entrepreneurship in Jharkhand and Constraints of SHG promotion in most backward regions, tribal dominated and left-wing influenced areas to seek immediate intervention.

Chapter - 8

Marginalization and Development

I would like to share with you some anthropological understandings of **marginal area** and **marginality**. Marginal area means the culture of communities which are at the periphery of a **culture area** and Culture area is a region which has a relatively similar way of living common to its component socio-economic systems and cultures. The centre of the culture area (which I will refer as "core") has uniform customs but its periphery (which I will refer as "margin") may be less homogenous. The concept is more relevant to the material culture than to other aspects of culture which we are focused here while using the term marginalization.

Marginality (internal) means referring to a group of people with a low level of culture-usually of a hunting, fishing and gathering type- who are surrounded by people of higher culture (that I call "core") as those living in 'deprived areas', where poor housing, inadequate social services, weak political voice and lack of decent work all combine to create an experience of marginalization.

However, there are various understandings of Marginalization and Development. To my mind, Marginalization is a socially constructed concept, and can depend on an idea of what is considered 'core'. In many developing countries, where most people do not enjoy an acceptable standard of living, defining what is 'core' is not a simple task, especially given the lack of the welfare state and a formalized labour market. Indeed, Marginalization can be structured around hierarchy, the exclusion of people on the basis of their race, caste or gender, may be viewed by the society excluding them from 'core'.

According to Canadian Council of Social Development (CCSD), "Ethnic disparities in the correctional system seem to be the result of both discrimination and biases in the system, as well as disproportionate offending within certain populations. However, research shows that those minority groups which are disproportionately involved in offending are those which are economically and socially disadvantaged, in many cases as a result of historical discrimination"[1].

In India the marginalized communities are rural poor, scheduled tribes and castes, manual workers in unorganized sectors etc. The marginalized people have very little or no participation in the development process. The initiatives are channeled through pre-existing power structure. Their conditions have remained unchanged over the centuries even after government initiatives implemented for their upward mobility. There has been serious thinking about the participation of marginalized communities in the process of development. Due to government failure of integrating them in the development process, an alternative has emerged in the form of civil society to evolve the strategy for empowerment of the marginalized people.

Marginalization is multidimensional, and can encompass a lack of access to employment, legal redress and markets; a lack of political voice; and poor social relationships. Therefore, it is not enough to examine these issues individually; the links between development and Marginalization must be explored. The causes of Marginalization have been attributed to the economic and social changes in free-market economies and to weaknesses in government policies and services because people, who are marginalized, to some extent, are also socially excluded and vulnerable.

What are the Marginalized excluded from?

How are we to understand the new social problems that have arisen as a result of the economic restructuring of advanced capitalist democracies since the mid-1970s? Three conflicting paradigms within which different meanings of Marginalization are embedded are – ***solidarity,specialization and monopoly***. These derive from the political ideologies of ***Republicanism, liberalism and social democracy.*** While the idea of Marginalization may help to focus attention on certain social categories, it may also distract attention from general rises in inequality and undermine universal approaches to social protection.

Development implies orderly movement of an organism or a social system from a lower level of functioning to a higher level of functioning and integration. Anthropologists generally considered development as a state of society providing for the security and necessities of its members, adopting itself continuously with the changing conception of good life. Development represents an increase in the capacities of the society to organize for its own objectives and to carry out its programmes more effectively.

The essential element here is the organization. India is a country with approximately 80% population living in the villages. It is therefore, important to develop the villages then only the country can be considered as developed country in the international arena. Tribal are integral part of Indian villages therefore, village development model is being suggested here for integrated development.

Despite deep dents made by forces of modernism, life in the developing nations continues to be governed by tradition. One feature of economic life in the traditional society is that it's closely integrated with other aspects of culture so much so that the methods of earning livelihood cannot possibly be modified without disturbing the manner of life in other crucial ways. [Mathur, 1995].

An examination of development projects indicated that while technical and economic issues are often adequately addressed in the project design, the people related variables frequently get relegated to the background. Thus, when people do not use irrigation water, which happen quite often, it may not be due to any engineering flows in the construction of channels; the trouble may be due to human factors initially ignored in the project design. Technically and economically sound projects are not necessarily socially sound as well. [Mathur, 1995].[3]

Understanding the people

Poverty focused development strategies can work only if planners try and understand the people for whom they plan development. It is not enough to produce plans, which look excellent on paper. Plans designed to assist development of the poor people must take account of their needs, and their capacity to absorb benefits from the development process. Most plan failures can be attributed not to technical imperfections in their formulation, but usually to a lack of understanding of socio – cultural realities on the part of both planners and project administrators. [Mathur, 1995] Here anthropology have great role to play.

Water is linked to the food supply and livelihood of south- Asia's rural poor in a myriad of complex ways: as a resource, water is increasingly seen as a key to many aspects of environmental sustainability and poverty reduction. The quality and availability of water directly impact on the quality of livelihoods, particularly for the poor. An entitlement to water is one of the most important factors in modern agricultural production, offering opportunities for improving livelihoods, particularly in rural areas. (Shah, 1998)

Assured supply of water, through irrigation or rainwater harvesting for rain fed agriculture, increases the food security of the rural poor. Food security implies increased agricultural production as well as sustained physical and economic access to balanced diets, safe drinking water, sanitation, basic health care and primary education. (MSSRF, 1996: in shah, 1998)

Since the independence of India, much is being done in the name of Tribal development to bring these millions of people in the mainstream of the advanced and modern cultural groups. Irrigation facilities were created for development of agriculture in 3rd and 4th five year plans and also completed by the government.

The development process has failed to end the deprivation faced by the marginalized communities in most of the developing nations. In fact, it has contributed to the social reproduction of marginalization. According to Human Development Report the marginalized people are emerged as victims of these processes of development. In every society there are some sections of people who are deprived of socio-economic opportunities for their sustenance and are victims of social, cultural and political exclusion.

Livelihood and land alienation: Land is the main natural endowment from which the tribes derive their sustenance and social status. 96% of the tribal depend solely on land for their livelihood even today. But things now have taken quite a different turn in matters of land use. The lands in tribal belts have acquired alarmingly a different meaning, purpose, and value in the eyes and minds of government and the non-tribal associates, the capitalists, the industrialists, the businessmen, professionals, and tradesmen because of the regions' mineral wealth, forests, and other natural resources.

Tribal right to land: The land ownership pattern among the tribes is changing very fast. It explodes the prevalent myth that tribes are becoming landless because of illegal transaction of land by land-brokers at the hands of non-tribes. It shows that the government intervention in the form of settlement of land, and the high purchasing power of the tribes has, in fact, increased their ownership over land. The study proves that tribes in Ranchi district have lost their lands to the extent of 6433.70 acres by way of transfers to non-tribes, land acquisitions for government projects, and Housing Corporation. But government has protected their interest by compensating the loss of land in the form of settlement of Land to the extent of 27850.44 acres of land in Ranchi district alone.

People's empowerment through grassroots level institutions: After the nationalization, commercial banks were expected to play pivotal role in improving the state of agriculture in the country. This could be through setting up more branches in rural areas, providing loan to small and marginal farmers, and ensuring timely flow of credit. A study revealed that substantial gap existed between target and achievement of commercial banks with respect to (a) branch establishment, (b) quantum of credit supply, (c) timely supply of credit, and (d) in improving the status of agriculture.

Access to education in the rural areas: Education as the Crucial Investment for Human Development For human welfare, freedom from ignorance, diseases and fear is as important as freedom from want. Education, health care, water and sanitation services and environment that promote health and social safety nets, which are required to provide such freedom, cannot be obtained easily by all through private action and, therefore, there is a need for public action. These facilities are collectively termed as 'social infrastructure' and are as critical as "physical infrastructure" for a widely shared inclusive development.

Economic development of rural groups: there is a marginal shift of working force from agriculture to non-agriculture sector due to marginalization of land holdings in Jharkhand. This has important implications. Those cultivators who had small piece of land had lost their land and converted into agricultural labourers. Most of them belong to tribal communities. The State is facing two major problems- poverty, and low rate of economic growth. The available evidence suggests strategies to bring about progressive diversification of the occupational structure in the secondary and tertiary sectors through the process of strengthening agriculture-industry linkages. Such linkages would help in increasing the demand for skilled ahead of rural employment demand. Thus, support programmes for skill development should be initiated in response to restructuring the rural production system. Following steps should be initiated immediately:

- Launch Entrepreneurship Training to Tribal Youth in marketable products and IT.

- Agro based Food processing, Dairy, Goat rearing, Pig rearing, Mushroom production, Beekeeping, Beehive box manufacturing, Production of Herbal pesticides, production of fishing trap, Detergent/soap manufacture,
- Cultivation and storage of medicinal plants, wooden handicraft, MANDAR(beating drum)production, Bamboo basket production, Broom making and marketing, Leaf mat, leaf bowl and leaf plate production etc.
- Provide financial package to establish home industries/business.
- Suitable rehabilitation package is required to check uprooting of Tribal.

Forest Management: To improve the condition of tribal, the control of natural resources should be with the people in the villages. Community based forest management in Jharkhand has emerged mainly in two forms-Indigenous Community Forest Management, and Joint Forest Management. These two types vary in composition, institutional rules, functioning of managing committee, modes of resolving the conflicts, and leadership pattern. Both social identity and participation were significantly higher in Indigenous Community Forest Management than the Joint Forest Management. Homogeneous community, units under participatory leadership evoked more social identity and people's participation. Members of Indigenous Community Forest Management had higher satisfaction with its institutional rules, managing committee's functioning and leadership pattern than Joint Forest Management.These factors of institutional governance directly enhanced social identity and also participation.

Integration is a way forward. Social integration has been defined as "the process of promoting the values, relations and institutions that enable all people to participate in social, economic and political life on the basis of equality of rights, equity and dignity" (UN Expert Group Meeting on Promoting Social Integration: Draft Summary, Finland, July 8-10 2008, p. 2). However, social integration can also imply integration on poor terms (like adverse incorporation), and cultural homogenization.

References

Mathur, Hari Mohan. Anthropology and Development in Traditional societies, Vikas publishing House Pvt. Ltd. New Delhi. 1995.

Sharma, V. P. Irrigated Agriculture and Challenges of development in Jharkhand, A K Hadar edited book, Societies and cultures in India, R.N Bhattacharya, Kolkata, pp. 123-138, 2008.

Sharma, Vijay Prakash. Thinking about Tribal Development through Integrated Village Development Model in Jharkhand, P. Dash Sharma edited book Livelihood and Health, Serial Publication, New Delhi, 2014.

UN Expert Group Meeting on Promoting Social Integration: Draft Summary, Finland, July 8-10 2008, p. 2.

Winick, Charles. N.d. Dictionary of Anthropology, PETER OWEN LIMITED, London, p. 39 and 343.

Chapter - 9

Strengthening Human Development Strategies for Education in Jharkhand

The new skill development programme launched by government of India and states enhances the aspirations of tribal but we need a proper implementation of this programme in Jharkhand. Education is one of the primary agents of transformation towards development. It's an activity, or a series of activities, or a process which either improves the immediate living conditions, social, economic, political, human, cultural, environmental, or increases the potential for future living. It plays an important role in bringing tangible benefits by developing the skills of the people. It expands livelihood opportunities and increases earning potential and thus helps in tackling the problem of poverty at large. The major role that education has been able to play is with regard to skill inculcation and skill improvement of the persons.

India has made huge progress in terms of increasing primary education attendance rate and expanding literacy to approximately two thirds of the population. However, education is still far behind developing countries such as China or Thailand. Most children never attend secondary schools. An optimistic estimate is that only one in five job-seekers in India have ever had any sort of vocational training.

Methods:

This paper is based on secondary data from published works and primary data collected through fieldwork in tribal villages of Jharkhand at different points of time in 2015-16 by the author using anthropological techniques like interview and observation followed by case studies.

Tribal development & education

It is a recorded truth by anthropologist that Women in tribal societies overpower male counterparts as workforce. Therefore, tribal development must be channelized through women's education. Development may be defined as a function of economic, social, education and cultural betterment of the people. Tribal women must be educated and trained in main stream education system so that they can further encourage their children to join the national development and education process.

Scheduled Tribes : Article 366 (25) of the Constitution of India refers to Scheduled Tribes as those communities, who are scheduled in accordance with Article 342 of the Constitution. This Article says thatonly those communities who have been declared as such by the Presidentthrough an initial public notification or through a subsequent amending Actof Parliament will be considered to be Scheduled Tribes. Article 342 provides for specification of tribes or tribal communities or parts of or groups within tribes or tribal communities which are deemed to be for the purposes of the Constitution the Scheduled Tribes in relation to that State or Union Territory. In pursuance of these provisions, the list of Scheduled Tribes are notified for each State or Union Territory and are valid only within the jurisdiction of that State or Union Territory and not outside. The list of Scheduled Tribes is State/UT specific and a community declared as a Scheduled Tribe in a State need not be so in another State. The inclusion of a community as a Scheduled Tribe is an ongoing process. The essential characteristics, first laid down by the Lokur Committee, for a community to be identified as Scheduled Tribes are –(a) indications of primitive traits; (b) distinctive culture; (c) shyness of contact with the community at large; (d) geographical isolation; and (e) backwardness. Tribal communities live, in various ecological and geo-climatic conditions ranging from plains and forests to hills and inaccessible areas. Tribal groups are at different stages of social, economic and educational development. While some tribal communities have adopted a mainstream way of life, at the other end of the spectrum, there are certain Scheduled Tribes, 75 in number known as Particularly Vulnerable Tribal Groups(PVTGs), who are characterized by (a) pre-agriculture level of technology; (b) stagnant or declining population; (c) extremely low literacy; and (d) subsistence level of economy.

Distribution of Tribes- The Scheduled Tribes are notified in 30 States/ UTs and the number of individual ethnic groups, etc. notified as Scheduled Tribes is 705. The tribal population of the country, as per 2011 census, is 10.43 crore, constituting 8.6% of the total population. 89.97% of them live in rural areas and 10.03% in urban areas. The decadal population growth of the tribal's from Census 2001 to 2011 has been 23.66% against the 17.69% of the entire population. (*Statistical Profile of Scheduled Tribes In India 2013*).

There are thirty-two different tribal communities residing in the Jharkhand State and they constitute 26.3 percent (6.6 million5) of the total population of the State. The average literacy rate of Jharkhand state is 54.13 percent, but among some tribal, particularly among the female, literacy rate is as low as 10 percent. Although the overall literacy rate among the STs has increased from 27.5 percent (1991 census) to 40.7 percent (2001 census) but despite this improvement, the literacy rate among the tribes is much below in comparison to that of all STs at the national level (47.1 percent). In Jharkhand, over all literacy rates among the STs, male and female (54 percent and 27.2 percent) are also considerably lower than those at the national level (59.2 percent & 34.8 percent). Increase in drop-out rates, falling learning levels and poor quality of education have also been general concerns and not only with regard to the tribal population as shown in the following tables-

Table - 1: Drop Out Rates of ST Students- 2010-11- Jharkhand

Class	*Boys*	*Girls*	*Total*
I-V	39.6	35	37.5
I-VIII	60.5	49.4	55.8
I-X	80.8	78.5	79.8

Source: Statistical Profile of Scheduled Tribes in India 2013, page 179, (*Source:* Statistics of School Education 2010-2011).

Table - 2: GROSS ENROLMENT RATIO (GER)- Scheduled Tribe Class I-V and Class VI-VIII IN Jharkhand

Class	*Boys*	*Girls*	*Total*
I-V	164.9	164.1	164.5
VI-VIII	84.0	80.8	82.4
I-X	115.5	112.4	114.0

Source: Statistical Profile of Scheduled Tribes in India 2013, Selected Educational statistics, MHRD, 2010-11.

Government Programmes for promotion of education for tribal

Under this programme several schemes namely scheme for Construction of Hostels for girls and boys, Establishment of Ashram schools, setting up of Educational Complexes in low literacy pockets for development of women's literacy, Post Matric Scholarship, Book Banks, Upgradation of

Merit, Coaching and allied schemes, scheme of Top Class Education, National Overseas Scholarship for students studying abroad, Rajiv Gandhi National Fellowship, Scheme of vocational training in tribal areas, etc. are covered. These schemes are meant for personality development through education which is the most effective instrument for empowering the tribals.

Administration of the 'The Scheduled Tribes and Other Traditional Forest Dwellers (Recognition of Forest Rights) Act, 2006', is vested in the MoTA. This radical legislation seeks to recognize and vest the forest rights and occupation in forest land in forest dwelling Scheduled Tribes and other traditional forest dwellers who have been residing in such forests for generations but whose rights on ancestral lands and their habitat were not adequately recognized in the consolidation of State forests during the colonial period as well as in independent India resulting in historical injustice to them. The Act was notified for operation with effect from 31.12.2007. The Scheduled Tribes and Other Traditional Forest Dwellers (Recognition of Forest Rights) Rules, for implementing the provisions of the Act, were notified on 1.1.2008. As per the Act, and the Rules notified there under, the responsibility for recognition and vesting of forest rights and distribution of land rights rests with the State Government. The whole process for determination of forest rights would start at the level of Gram Sabha, which will be scrutinized at Sub-Divisional Level Committee, after which the District Level Committee will approve/award forest rights.

Since the beginning of the First Five Year Plan, the Planning Commission, various Committees and Commissions and the Ministry of Tribal Affairs (since its inception in 1999) have proposed and developed plans and policies from time to time to address the issues of the Constitutional safeguards, Acts and Regulations relating to protection of the interests of tribals in forests and trade, etc. As a result, several institutions have evolved in the States for implementation of such schemes and programmes. These are : Autonomous District Councils in the North East, Integrated Tribal Development Agencies (ITDA), Integrated Tribal Development Programmes (ITDP), Tribal Development (TD) Blocks and Tribal Research Institutes (TRIs).

In recent years the schemes/programmes are focused on three crucial aspects of integrated development of Tribal population namely: infrastructure, community and personality development. There are ten central sector schemes, four centrally sponsored schemes and two special area programmes. The important highlights of these schemes /programmes are:-

(i) **Special assistance** is provided under **Article 275(1)** for promoting the welfare of STs and for raising the level of administration of scheduled areas to that of the rest of the State. The funding under Article 275(1) of the Constitution is basically focused on infrastructure and community development in the remote tribal areas to bring them at par with other areas of the State.

(ii) **Special Central Assistance to Tribal Sub Plan** is an additive to the State Plans in areas where the State Plan Provisions are not normally sufficient for rapid economic development of the Tribals. Till the end of IX Five Year Plan it was meant for filling up the critical gaps in the family based income generation activities of the tribal sub plan, but from the X Five Year Plan the objective and scope has been expanded to cover employment-cum-income generation activities and infrastructure incidental thereto. The ultimate objective of this extension is to boost the demand based income generation programmes to raise the economic and social status of tribals. 30% of the beneficiaries of this scheme are to be women and priority of funding is accorded to the neglected tribals living in forest villages. An additional Central Assistance of Rs. 500.00 crores was provided as a one time assistance during 2009-10 to the various State Governments for educational development of children in Scheduled V areas and naxal affected areas. Out of this amount, an amount of Rs. 442.23 crores was released upto 31.12.09. However, no budget provision has been made for 2010-11 for this.

Funding of Tribal Development Programmes

Funds for socio-economic development of tribal people are sourced from the following:-

(i) Tribal Sub-Plan component of the State Plan;

(ii) Special Central Assistance to Tribal Sub-Plan;

(iii) Sectoral programmes of Central Ministries/ Departments, and;

(iv) Institutional finance.

The State Governments are required to quantify the funds from the state plan for tribal areas development in proportion to the percentage of tribal population in the States. Similarly, Central Ministries are also required to quantify the funds from sectoral programmes for tribal development in proportion to the percentage of the tribal population in the country. These funds, comprising the Tribal Sub-Plan (TSP) are to be used for implementing development programmes in the tribal areas, primarily for the Scheduled Tribes, in the fields of education, health, agriculture, horticulture, small industries, artisans and other income generating activities. Recently the Ministry of Finance have instructed all Central Ministries to reflect the component under the Tribal Sub-plan as a distinctive schedule in the Demand for Grants of the concerned Ministry from the Budget of 2011-12 and that the Planning Commission should have a MOU with all Central Ministries on the level of share earmarked for TSP in the Annual Plan of the Ministry for 2011-12.

It is important to mention here that the Ministry of Tribal Affairs supports supplements and facilitates the efforts of the Line Ministries, States and the institutions/organizations working for the welfare of the tribals.

Need for a Strategic Plan

Yet, the measure of development indices of Scheduled Tribes continues to lag significantly behind the other communities. The level of rural poverty amongst the Scheduled Tribes on an all-India basis as per Planning Commission's estimates in 2004-05 is 47.20 percent and urban poverty is 33.30 percent, both levels significantly higher than the average across different sections. The spread of poverty is concentrated in tribal dominant states such as Chhatisgarh (54.20), Jharkhand (54.20), Madhya Pradesh (58.60), Mharashtra (56.60), Orissa (75.60) and West Bengal (42.40).

In terms of literacy levels, the gap between the ST and others remains significant. While the all-India average literacy was 64.84 percent in 2001 (Male – 75.26%; Female – 53.67%), the level for ST was 47.10 percent (Male – 59.17%; Female – 34.76%). Though the gap narrowed when compared to literacy levels over a 40 – year period, the high drop-out rates amongst STs is reflective of the persistent and continuing low literacy levels amongst the tribals. The MoTA has been implementing the post-matric scholarship scheme for the ST along with several other merit and income based scholarships for higher studies. These, however, have not been able to address the high drop-out rates at primary, elementary and secondary levels that are feeder to higher studies.

A study conducted at the behest of MoTA on the Tribal Sub Plan programme in the states of Andhra Pradesh, Maharashtra and Madhya Pradesh reveals that TSP did not receive adequate funding in Maharashtra and Madhya Pradesh in proportion to the tribal population in these states. It also points to a plethora of agencies involved in different schemes for tribal welfare without any convergence, thus dissipating the funds earmarked for development of this activity.

Discussion

On the basis of several studies and field discussions it is clear that Persistently poor educational attainment for the tribal in Jharkhand is a result due to poor quality of life and socio-economic deprivation suffered by the majority of tribal population. The issue of inadequate trained, skilled and motivated teachers for the education of the tribal must be addressed on urgent basis. Despite the various programs in place the learning gaps between the tribal and general population has been increasing as also the gap in the drop-out rate. Increase in drop-out rates, falling learning levels and poor quality of education have also been general concerns and not only with regard to the tribal population.

Suggestion

Jharkhand must work rigorously for Strengthening Human Development Strategies for Education in Jharkhand through following Short and Medium Term strategies to address the problem of education-

A. Short Term Strategy-

1. Providing incentives to households to send their children to school.
2. Filling up vacant positions with teachers with subject specific knowledge for upper primary and secondary schools, additional teachers to ease the burden of multi-grade teaching in single teacher schools, adequate female teachers and teachers who understand the local tribal language and are sensitive to the contextual culture

B. Medium Term strategy-

1. Upgrading Education Guarantee Schemes (EGS) into primary schools in a phased manner
2. Providing the minimum pre-service and regular in-service training to teachers without formal teacher training
3. Analyzing the tenure, qualification requirements, standardization, selection and appointment and pre-service and in-service training of Para-teachers

4. Setting up of the State Institute of Education Management and Training and strengthening the links between all these support systems
5. Periodic evaluations to provide technical support for SIERT and State Institute of Educational Management and Training (SIEMAT) in curriculum revision, textbook development, and training of trainers at the district levels, research and evaluation.
6. Addressing under spending of Sarva Shiksha Abhiyan (SSA) allocations and identifying activities using the innovative grants in SSA aimed at introducing state specific interventions
7. Promote public–private partnerships, especially at the secondary level since 10 per cent of the total schools are under grants-in-aid
8. Increase the private institutions under grants-in-aid
9. Expansion of the vocational education sector and
10. Develop additional strategy for the followings-
    (a) Address the persisting gaps in the development of tribal areas in order to bridge completely the difference by 2020 the vis-à-vis other areas despite six decades of targeted planned development by creating policies and programmes that would enable the tribal areas and STs to garner the benefits from the overall economic growth in the country and its integration into the global economy;
    (b) Improve harnessing of the abundant natural resources in the tribal areas to bring direct benefits to the STs in line with the value of the resources;
    (c) Fill-in the gaps in service deficient tribal areas in sectors such as rights, education, health, drinking water, livelihood and social security through the efforts of Voluntary Organisations, State Govts/ UTs, and Central Ministries;
    (d) Create livelihood supporting infrastructure that is relevant, of excellent quality and is in convergence with other infrastructure development schemes of Government of India/ State Govts by helping State Governments to better design Conservation-cum-Development (CCD) Plans for Particularly Vulnerable Tribal Groups (PTGs) and proposals under Article 275(1) Proviso of Constitution of India.
    (e) Redress through requisite capacity building, dissemination of credible information and awareness generation the growing

alienation amongst tribals that has resulted in serious law and order problems threatening the core of democratic structure;

(f) Strengthen through transfer of resources, human resource development and hand-holding, established, but moribund, institutions like ADCs, ITDA/ITDP to enable them to actively plan and implement schemes and programmes for rapid development of tribals and tribal areas envisaged by 2020;

(g) Introduce greater decentralization of service delivery and finances by facilitating State Governments and other lower tiers to upgrade the existing administration in the Tribal Areas;

(h) Ensure better targeting of service delivery and outcomes through targeted skill development and capacity building for government functionaries and agencies;

(i) Shift the focus of the MoTA from its existing role as a disburser of funds for a set of schemes to assume additionally the role of coordination and monitoring of the plans and programmes of line ministries as well as State Govts/ UTs Administration to incorporate the specificities of tribal needs and, therefore, build in differential norms and delivery modalities compared to the rest of the country.

(j) Bring about efficiency and transparency in the functioning of the Ministry through use of technology in implementation, monitoring and evaluation; and by building a National Tribal Information System for collection and dissemination of all information connected with development and welfare of the tribals and tribal areas;

Conclusion

Persistently poor educational attainment for the tribal is a result due to poor quality of life and socio-economic deprivation suffered by the majority of tribal population. The issue of inadequate trained, skilled and motivated teachers for the education of the tribal must be addressed on urgent basis. Despite the various programs in place the learning gaps between the tribal and general population has been increasing as also the gap in the drop-out rate. Increase in drop-out rates, falling learning levels and poor quality of education have also been general concerns and not only with regard to the tribal population.

Lack of proper monitoring and evaluation mechanism adds to the problem. There is a need for attitudinal changes at all levels towards education for tribal children and child centered learning in general. Due to diversity of languages the need for multilingual education is of intrinsic value (social, cognitive and developmental) of and hence mother-tongue based education is recommended. There is a need for concrete outcome based planning from the ground level if we want to bring development in tribal societies of Jharkhand. Jharkhand must work rigorously for Strengthening Human Development Strategies for Education in Jharkhand through suggested Short and Medium Term strategies to address the problem of education in tribal area.

References

1. Jharkhand: Addressing the challenges of inclusive Development, World Bank, 2008.
2. Selected Educational statistics, MHRD, 2010-11.
3. Strategic Plan - 2012 – 2017,(Revised), Ministry of Tribal Affairs, Govt. of India Statistical profile of scheduled tribes in India 2013, Ministry of Tribal Affairs,Statistics division, Government of India, www.tribal.nic.in,
4. Report No. 36437 IN of World Bank, 2008.
5. Sharma. Vijay Prakash, Traditional knowledge of indigenous people as part of Women's Education, 44th National Seminar on Indigenous knowledge system and sustainable livelihood for the tribal, December 7-8, 2015, ISRAA, BIDISA.

Chapter - 10

Cultivation in Jharkhand: Need for Management of Water and Land Resources

The tribal major state of Jharkhand is rich in mineral and natural resources that have been vastly exploited by the state. The tribal though have very little access to these resources and live in utter poverty. They depend mostly on agriculture for their livelihood. The main crop that is sown is paddy, which is heavily dependent on rainfall. Once paddy is harvested no other crop is grown because of lack of irrigational facilities. Only a few cash crops are grown if water is available for irrigation. Thus, management of water and land resources for cultivation is essential for water based livelihood development.

The purpose of this study was to identify Water resources in the villages and suggest probable solutions to deal with the lack of irrigational facilities The intervention in this regard should be done after consultation with the experts to uplift the economic conditions of the villagers especially the tribal.

Methodology

- Initial PRA and sample survey work were carried out in 12 villages in each of the two blocks of Ranchi district namely Bundu, Namkom,
- Sample size: 10% of total beneficiaries from 12 villages of Bundu and Namkom block of Ranchi District in Jharkhand.
- A questionnaire cum schedule was developed and used. The analysis conducted through specially developed software package for computer.

- Total 180 households from following thirteen villages were covered under this survey.

Bundu Block

1. Kanchi
2. Heth Kanchi
3. Gosaidih
4. Badkolma
5. Tau
6. Alna
7. Neori
8. Madhukama
9. Gutuhatu

Namkom Block

1. Haratu
2. Tati
3. Silwai
4. Lalganj (Kanke)

Survey Result

Village profile of the Block Bundu

Village : Kanchi

The village Kanchi is located along the river Kanchi. It is situated nearly 45 kms from Ranchi. It lies west of the NH 33. The village is approximately two kms from the national highway. The geographical area is nearly 531.88 hectares that includes both the cultivable as well as forest land. The village is a mix of various communities like Mundas, Lohras, Swansies and Sahus. The tribal population is dominant in the village with 116 households belonging to the schedule tribes. The soil is fertile and agriculture is the main occupation of the people. The river Kanchi flows in the south of the village and dries up during the summer months. Thus people depend on monsoon for cultivation.

Village : Heth Kanchi

The village Heth Kanchi is situated approximately two and a half kms west from the NH 33. The village is adjacent to Kanchi village. The river Kanchi flows in the south of the village which forms the major source of irrigation for the people. The geographical spread of the village is approximately 750 acres. The village consists of Lohras, Mundas, Swansies, and some general households. The soil is basically Red soil. The village is mostly agro based and agriculture is highly dependent on rainfall. The village also has the advantage of forest area but is not very dense.

Village : Gosaidih

The village Gosaidih is situated along NH 33. It lies in the east of the national highway. It is nearly 48 kms from the capital. The village falls under Kanchi Panchayat in Bundu block. The total geographical spread of the village is 123.5 hectares. The cultivable area is 114.81 hectares, forest area is 1.1 hectares and wasteland is 4.95 hectares. The total population of the village is 676 with 346 males and 330 females. The village consists of Mundas, Ahirs, Tanties, Adhikaries and Nais community. The tribals dominate the village. The soil is red laterite soil and people are mostly farmers. Agriculture is very much dependent on rainfall. There is also a dam in the eastern side of the village which is also is source of irrigation for the people.

Village : Alna

Alna is situated in the east of NH 33. The village is located approximately five kms from the national highway. The village falls under Tau Panchayat in Block Bundu in Ranchi district. The total geographical area of the village is 230.63 hectares that includes cultivable area and wasteland. The cultivable area and wasteland in the village is 183.09 hectares and 40.96 hectares respectively. The village is relatively small with households consisting of Munda and Swansi community. People are dependent on agriculture for their livelihood.

Village : Tau

The village Tau is situated in the east of Ranchi Jamshedpur highway. It is nearly three and a half kms from the NH 33. The total geographical area of the village is 529.03 hectares. The cultivable area and wasteland in the village is 374.44 hectares and 85.08 hectares respectively. The village is dominated by communities such as Oraons, and some households of general communities. The soil is rich and fertile making the land fit for the growth of paddy. The villagers are generally agriculturists and depend on monsoon for the cultivation of the crops.

Village : Badkalma

The village Badkalma lies to the left of the NH 33 that runs in the east west direction of the village. The village is in Madhukama Panchayat in Bundu block of Ranchi district. The village is approximately two and a half kms away from the highway. The total geographical spread of the village is 262.77 hectares including cultivable area, wasteland and forest area. Forest land fringes the western side of the village and covers an area of 29.29

hectares. The village consists of Mundas, Lohras, and few other communitiesof general households. There are 298 males and 339 females in the village thus making a total population of 637 people. People practice agriculture for their livelihood.

Village : Gutuhatu

The village lies to the left of the NH 33 that runs in the north south direction from the village. The village is spread in an area of 406.72 hectares that includes cultivable and wasteland. The village falls in Kanchi Panchayat in Bundu block of Ranchi district. The village is surrounded by River Argu on all three sides barring the northern side of the village. The village population consists of Mundas, Oraons, Mahlis and Lohras. The village is agriculture based and people are dependent on rainfall for cultivation.

Village : Madhukama

The village Madhukama lays approximately 50 kms from Ranchi on the Ranchi Jamshedpur Highway. The village is situated west of NH 33. The total geographical area of the village is 149.94 hectares. The forest area is on the western side of the village. The population of the village consists of Munda, Yadav, Mahto, Lohra, and Gonghu households. The people are basically agriculturists and are dependent on rainfall for agriculture.

Village : Neori

Neori village is located to the west of NH 33. The village is in Tau Panchayat in Bundu block. The total spread of the village is 200 acres that includes both the Don land and the Tanr land. The Don area in the village is approximately 60 acres whereas the Tanr area is 100 acres. The households in the village are 14 that comprise Oraons and Mundas. The main occupation of the people is agriculture that is dependent on rainfall.

Village profile of the Block Namkom

Village : Tati

The village Tati is situated in Namkom block of Ranchi district in Tatisilwai Panchayat. It is located nearly 15 kms north of Ranchi district. The village is close to Ranchi Purulia Road and lies in the west of the road. A *kaccha* road leads to the village. The total population of the village is 10,496. Women population is 4,786 and the male population is 5,710. The total schedule tribe population of the village is 401, schedule caste is 380 and other community in the village is 9715. The village mostly consists of

Brahmins, Mahtos, Oraons, Dhobies and Ghasi community. The total area of the village is 3200 sq. kms out of which 2500 acre land is cultivable land. Nearly 90% of this cultivable land is Don and only 10% is Tanr land. The soil is mainly Red and Black type. The main crop that is sown in the village is paddy. River Swarnarekha touches the boundary of the village. It flows nearly half a kilometer in the south to north direction of the village.

Village : Haratu

Haratu village lies in Namkom block of Ranchi district. The village is in the northern direction nearly 10 kms from Ranchi on the Ranchi Purulia Road. It is at a distance of nearly half a kilometer from this NH 75. The total population of the village is 1944, out of which male and female population is 1057 and 887 respectively. Schedule tribe in the village is 744, schedule caste is 49 and 1151 belong to other community. Oraon, Mundas, Lohras, and Mahtos form the main community of the village. The total geographical area of the village is 2.361 sq kms. At nearly a distance of half a kilometer from the village there is a forest area which is spread in an area of 0.322 sq kms. The soil type is Red and Black. Paddy is the major crop hat is sown in the village. The river Swarnrekha is in the north of the village and flows from east to west at nearly a kilometer away from the village.

Village : Lalganj

Lalganj falls under Sugnu Panchayat in Kanke block in Ranchi district. It lies in the north east direction from Ranchi at a distance of 12 kms on the Ranchi Purulia Road. It falls in the west of the road at a distance of one and a half kilometers away from the road. The total population of the village is 1900. 90% of the total population of the village belongs to schedule tribe and the rest of the population consists of Mahtos, Sahus and Barikh community. The total geographical area of the village is 800 acres out of which 725 acre land is cultivable. The cultivable land includes 85% Don and 15% Tanr land. The soil is mostly Red. Paddy is the main crop in the village. Swarnrekha River flows in the east of the village at a distance of a kilometer from the village. The flow of the river is from south to north. The river touches the border of the village.

Research Findings-

Social Demography

- **Population composition:** Out of total respondents 59.49%were male and 40.50% were female.

- **Marriage status:** out of total population, 62.13% were married, 37.48% unmarried and 0.37% were widow.
- **Family size:** Average family size is 4.
- **Religion:** 96.8% Hindu and 3.19% were Christians.
- **Language:** 54% speaks Hindi and 45.74%speaks Mundari, Sadri and Panch- Pargania dialect as mother tongue.
- **Hose types:** Majority of houses i.e.53% are kacha, 36%tiled and only10.63% are pucca with concrete roofs.
- **Education:** 56.98%people was educated.
- **Electricity:** Though all villages under survey were electrified but irregular power supply is the great problem for villagers.

Economic condition

- **Land Holding Pattern:** Most of the people i.e. 88.82 % were marginal farmers having less than five acres of land. 9.57% owns land between five to ten acres, 1.59% had more than ten acres of land. 0.53% registered them as landless.
- **Average House hold Annual income:** 65.95% said that their annual income runs below rupees five thousand. 21.27% said that they earn rupees five to ten thousand annually, 12.76% said that they earn above ten thousand per annum.
- **Source of Income:** Agriculture was the main source of income for 86.17% respondents, 8.57% were daily labourer, 2.12% were in service and 3.19% are self employed through small business activities.
- **Average Household Annual Expenditure:** Majority of respondents i.e. 65.44% said that their annual expenditure is below Rupees five thousand, 27.27% said that their annual income comes in between Rupees 5000.00 to 10000.00. Only 13.29% respondents incur annual expenditure above Rupees 10000.00.
- **Average House Hold Monthly Income:** Average household monthly income of respondents was Rs. 1027.97 and expenditure was Rs. 1017.17. Total balance saving comes to Rs. 37.06 per month. This is the income in addition to crops for livelihood.
- **Occupation:** 33.83% respondents were agriculturists, 13.83% are labourer, and 16.10% housewives & self-employment were very less 0.5% & 012% respectively.

- **Employment:** Only 0.37% were employed in industrial sector.
- **Education:** Education is good 56.98% were educated only 12.95% uneducated but literate.
- **Political awareness:** Karmu Mahto in the area was popular leader favoured by 17.07%. Next to him was Ramjatan Mahto 9.57% followed by Kashinath & Kokil Munda 8.351% each.

0.53% respondents identified a lady named Nulian Devi as leader in their area.

Parties Name		%age
BJP	-	15.95
Cong	-	1.06
AJSU	-	1.59
CPI	-	1.06
JMM	-	7.97
Not Replied	-	69.14

- **Women Status:** -Women's status was considered low by 89.36%, High by 3.19% respondents. Women's role was considered to be supportive by 92.02% respondents and only 0.53% said that their status is authoritative.

  45.21% women work for cow-dung preparation in addition to household daily chores such as cooking, animal husbandry, fuel collection, stitching etc.

Discussion

Now days, agriculture has become expensive due to use of chemical fertilizers, high yielding variety seeds, pesticides etc. The agriculturist tribal communities under irrigated agriculture area purchase the seed and fertilizer from market. They have adopted new technology of diesel or electric pump sets for irrigating their lands in place of 'Latha-kudi'. But the small group still depends on this old technique. Their agricultural implements like plough, Juath, Harish, Henga, Khurpi, Sickle, axe, hammer, kudal, chain etc. are the traditional one. The tribal in the area does not have continuous agricultural activities because of hill terrain and less involvement of many tribal communities belonging to hill cultivation type.

Irrigated agricultural activities are lesser among tribal communities than the non tribals in the Ranchi district of which these blocks are the part.

As per government record only 8% of its area is under irrigated agriculture so most areas are dependent on rainfall for agriculture and only such crops are grown which are easily produced based on natural conditions. Though, during recent years, development of minor irrigation schemes and river valley projects have allowed cultivators to grow some other crops using ground and surface water. Recently the interest towards Rabi crops has increased. Areas having comparatively homogeneous land and irrigation facility have higher percentage of Rabi crops.

Recommendations

There is an urgent need for management of water Resources in the area for cultivation. The following steps should be taken on urgent basis to enhance the Economic conditions of people of the area at the block level by the government.

- Tank and well irrigation have great prospect in the Munda & Oraon areas. It is remarkable to note that water table in this area passes just below the Don land.
- The govt. drugged a good number of tanks on Tanr land. But these tanks become dry just after the rainy season and practically they are useless for villagers.
- The minor irrigation projects have failed in the area because the plans of such tanks could not take the local hydraulic condition into consideration.
- Some check dams constructed by Govt. funding through NGOs functioned well till the project period under ITDP schemes but become non functional after intervention period. Such projects should be handed over properly to village committees after proper training into management procedures.
- It is worthwhile to make arrangement for the storage of water on plain area it self through rain water harvesting.
- Some rivers can be dammed, some reservoirs can be made in the vicinity of natural wells and tanks etc. can be dug in relation to the water table.
- Water from these tanks and reservoirs can be made accessible to the Tanr land with the help of pumps which should be provided by the govt. on easy credit system and installment payment.

- Some check dams and lift irrigations established by NGO Ram Krishna Mission in Angara block are good example how people are using it for benefit through people's participation. The yield has not only gone up but double crops are raised. These facilities are functioning well where as govt. constructed schemes have become non functional.

GRAPHS

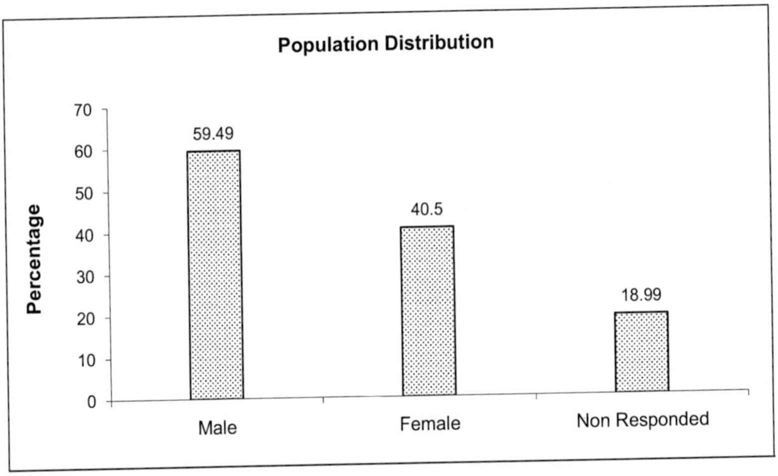

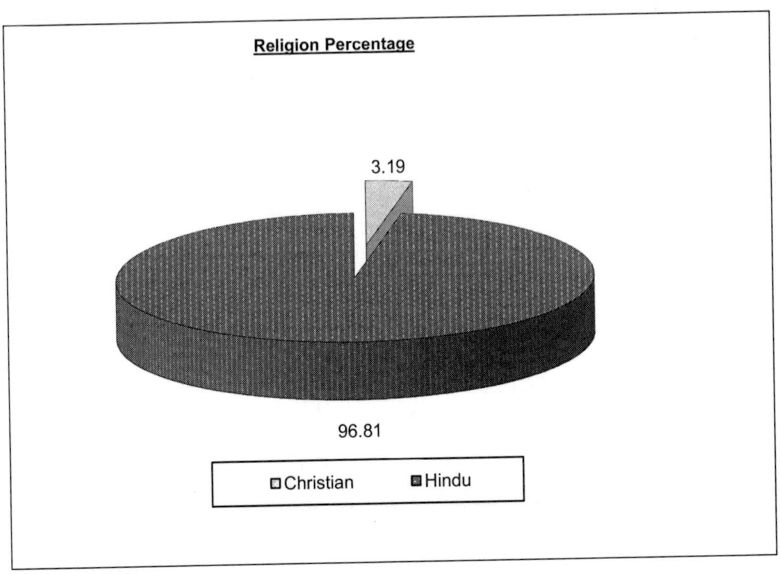

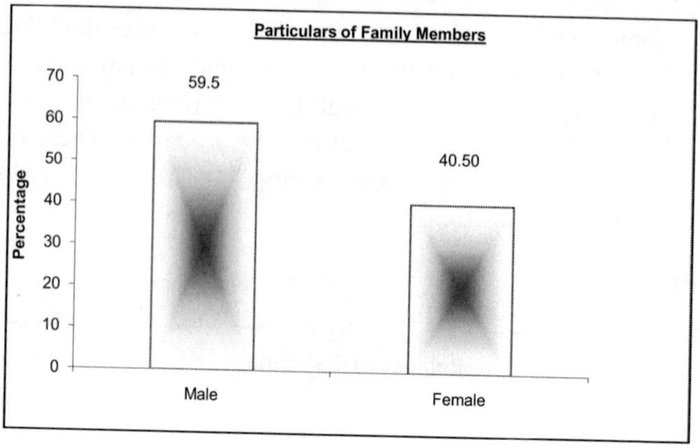
Particulars of Family Members
Percentage
70
60
50
40
30
20
10
0
59.5
40.50
Male
Female

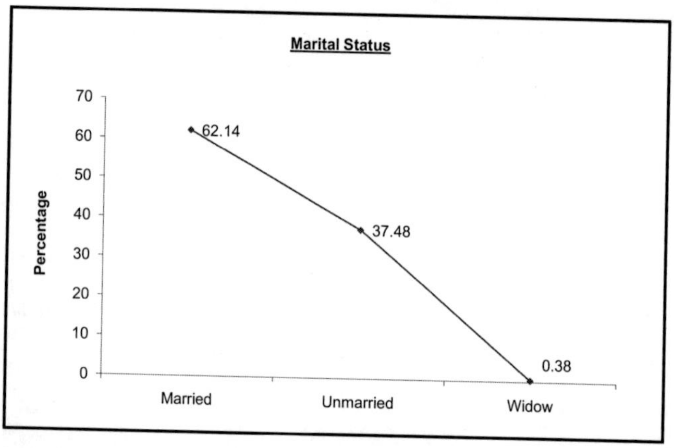
Marital Status
Percentage
70
60
50
40
30
20
10
0
62.14
37.48
0.38
Married
Unmarried
Widow

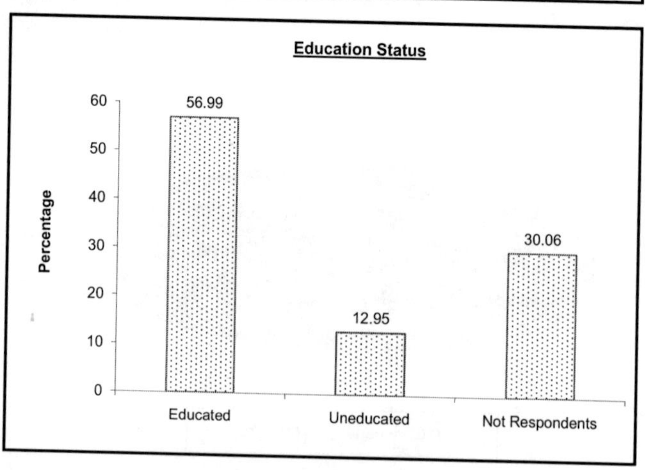
Education Status
Percentage
60
50
40
30
20
10
0
56.99
12.95
30.06
Educated
Uneducated
Not Respondents

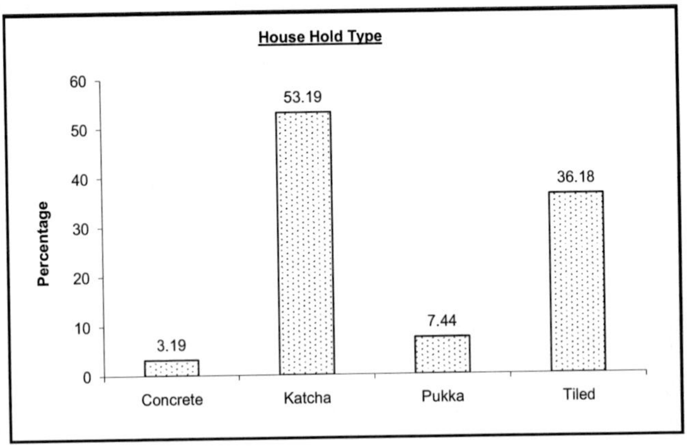
House Hold Type
Percentage
60
50
40
30
20
10
0
3.19
53.19
7.44
36.18
Concrete
Katcha
Pukka
Tiled

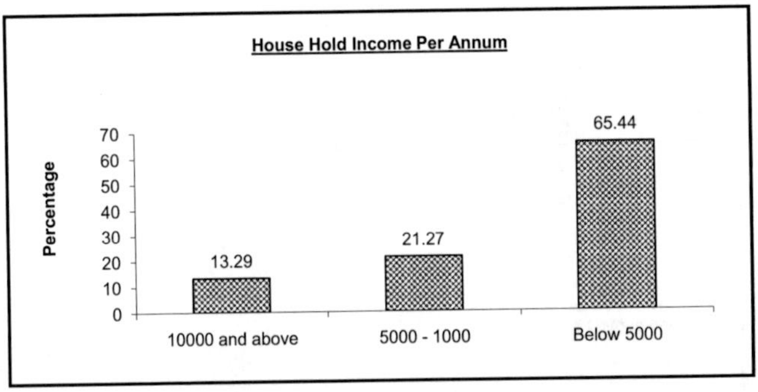
House Hold Income Per Annum
Percentage
70
60
50
40
30
20
10
0
13.29
21.27
65.44
10000 and above
5000 - 1000
Below 5000

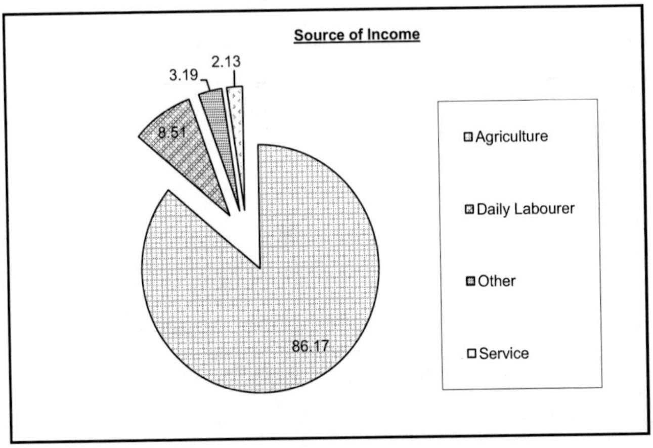
Source of Income
3.19
2.13
8.51
86.17
Agriculture
Daily Labourer
Other
Service

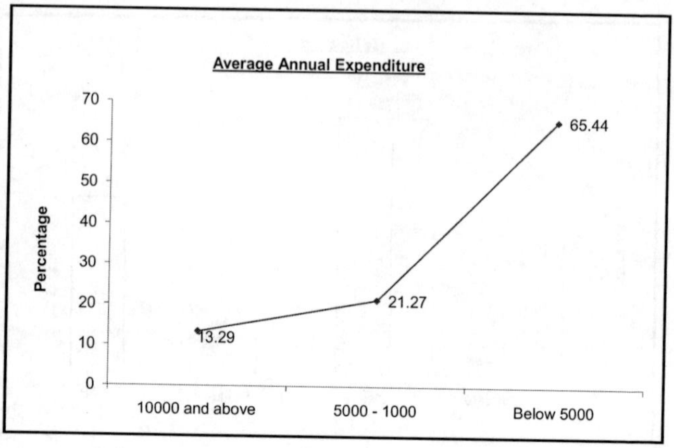
Average Annual Expenditure
Percentage
70
60
50
40
30
20
10
0
65.44
21.27
13.29
10000 and above
5000 - 1000
Below 5000

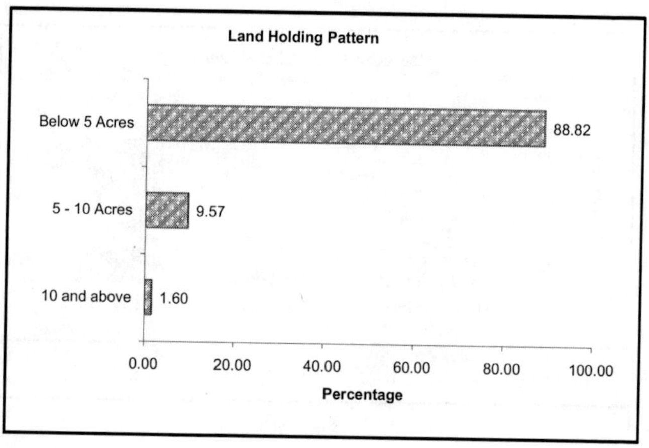
Land Holding Pattern
Below 5 Acres
88.82
5 - 10 Acres
9.57
10 and above
1.60
0.00
20.00
40.00
60.00
80.00
100.00
Percentage

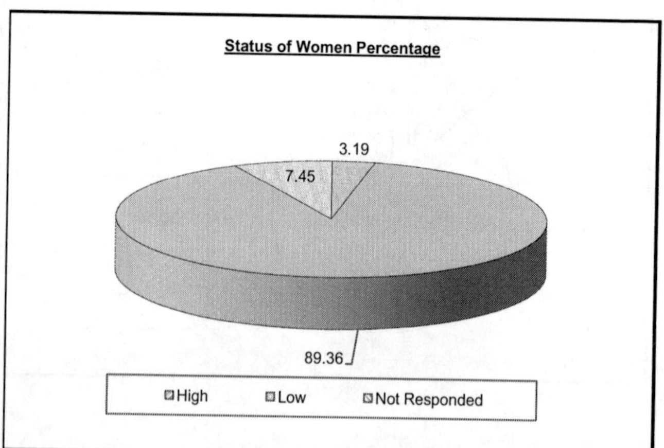
Status of Women Percentage
3.19
7.45
89.36
High
Low
Not Responded

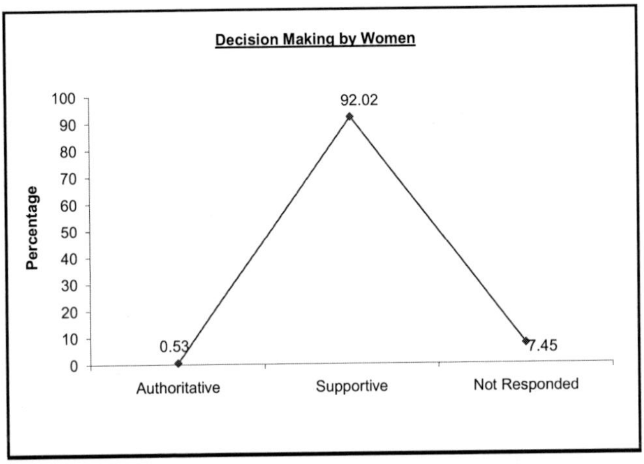
Decision Making by Women
Percentage
100
90
80
70
60
50
40
30
20
10
0
92.02
0.53
7.45
Authoritative
Supportive
Not Responded

Chapter - 11

People's participation and food security

India is a moving example of how food sufficiency at the aggregate level has not translated into food security at the household level. The thrust of all the Food Programmes run by the government or NGOs should shift to people's participation to bring the hungry, malnourished, and vulnerable within the ambit of human development.

Today, on the threshold of 64momentous years of Independence, the nation is justifiably proud of its myriad achievements. Among these is the remarkable success in eliminating widespread famines and the impressive increases in food production. Nonetheless, there is a long road to be travelled before the vision of a truly food secure India is achieved.

Recent years have seen the economy booming and growth rates have been among the highest in the world. The flip side, however, is that one in every five Indians suffers from overt or covert hunger. "Hunger," as stated by Amartya Sen and Jean Dreze, is "intolerable in the modern world" in a way it could not have been in the past, because it is "so unnecessary and unwarranted." India is a poignant example of how food sufficiency at the aggregate level has not translated into food security at the household level. A staggeringly large number of undernourished — about 214 million people — is chronically food insecure. Many more, varyingly about 40 million, are exposed to natural disasters. About 50 per cent of children (mostly tribal and rural) are undernourished and stunted, 23 per cent have a low birth weight and 68 out of 1000 die before the age of one year. There is a high prevalence of anaemia and other micronutrient deficiencies. (Bordignon, 2007)

The state of India's food security is worsening by the year. The cost of food items is increasing rapidly, making them unaffordable to a majority of the people. Added to these woes is the short supply of pulses and edible oils, which forces the Central government to import them.

Pulses play a critical role in the diet of the people of India, where large sections are vegetarians. Protein plays a key role in the human diet. It is the body-building nutrient that develops muscles and is responsible for body strength, endurance and productivity at the workplace.

It is established that a human body requires a daily intake of about 50 gm of protein. While people in the developed countries and most of the developing countries have a satisfactory intake of protein, in India the per capita daily intake is only about 10 gm. This endangers health and work performance.

Proteins are amino acids. Out of the 22 amino acids required in the human diet, the body supplies 14. The remaining eight have to come from food. If all the eight amino acids are present in a single food item, it is called a complete protein food.

Since all proteins from animal sources are complete proteins, it is easy to meet the dietary protein requirements of non-vegetarians. However, the main sources of protein for vegetarians are leguminous plants — to which pulses belong. In general, pulses have lower concentrations of protein than animal sources. Besides, none of the pulses — except soybeans — are complete proteins. Therefore, combinations of two or more pulses are needed in a vegetarian diet. Dairy products, which are complete proteins, may also be used to supplement pulse proteins in vegetarian diets.

Given the important role that pulses play in the human diet, their availability needs to be increased indigenously. The common belief that without new high-yielding varieties the country will have to continue importing pulses and edible oils to meet the requirements is not true.

The possibility of improving productivity per acre by an order of two to three times using existing varieties has been demonstrated time and again in grower-fields in India. However, it is not done just by following current production practices but through the adoption of entirely new but simple and farmer-friendly technologies and tools that are now not available to Indian farmers.

The underlying problem of Indian agriculture that threatens food security is extremely low productivity. For example, in the case of rice it is only a third of what has been achieved elsewhere. Cotton productivity is only a sixth of what has been achieved in developed countries. The situation is no different in the case of other crops. In order to progress, the mindset with regard to the following two factors needs to change:

1. It is not the farmer who makes the food: he is only a facilitator. Food is actually made by plants. Therefore, it is important to understand the requirements of plants and supply them without restrictions in order for plants to deliver food. Since plants do not talk, their needs are understood through research and experimentation. As indicated by Dr. R.S. Paroda, a former Director-General of the Indian Council of Agricultural Research (ICAR), our agriculture scientists will not by themselves be able to cope with the food security challenges that face the country.

   The current policy of pampering farmers with subsidies will get us nowhere in terms of improving productivity. This is well understood not only in developed countries but also in developing African countries like Malawi. Malawi was a basket case of poverty, malnutrition and food shortage. Crop productivity improvements have taken it to the point where the country now exports its surplus food to neighboring poor countries.

   The lesson India has to learn is that instead of subsidising food supply to the people, the plants need subsidised food such as fertilizers and other inputs in order for them to produce the food to achieve food security.

2. The mindset that assumes that breeding is the solution to all maladies has to change. Nurturing of plants is several times more important in crop productivity improvement than hybrid seeds per se. A hybrid variety will not produce if planted in non-fertile beach soil. But it will produce several times more if planted in fertile soil.

   Brazil learnt this lesson years ago and stopped financing breeding for new varieties. Instead, it scours countries around the world and selects promising varieties to test their adaptability to Brazilian climatic conditions and then provides funding just to do that. It has taken stem cuttings of black pepper varieties from Kerala and spent money and effort on crop production practices. Now Brazil's pepper yield is 1,500 kg an acre compared to India's average of 350 kg an acre, the lowest among all pepper-producing countries.

India has about 50 million acres of irrigated land and is second only to the United States with 60 million acres. In the U.S. it is possible to raise only one crop a year due to weather constraints. However, many areas in India have the potential to raise three crops a year, provided we learn how to sustain the fertility of the soil. This will be equal to 150 million acres of irrigated land. At the present time our system of monitoring soil fertility and maintaining it is flawed and needs urgent attention. We cannot just bury our heads in soil as ostriches may do.

According to Dr. Lux Lakshmanan, Director, California Agriculture Consulting Service, Davis, California. Finally, we have facilities now in place in Tamil Nadu to adopt new crop production technologies and tools, where crop productivity is routinely maintained at 300 per cent to 500 per cent more per acre than the average in India. We are now in the process of developing infrastructure for the rapid propagation of these highly cost-effective crop production technologies across the country

The government claims that it has attained self suffciency in food grain production.What is the measure of Self Sufficency, Whether it is Quality or Quantity. The claim of record breaking food grain production will not feed the hungry stomach of starving million Indians. The reports of large quantity of food grains getting rotted present a dsymal picture in the backdrop of hungry peole. Doing simple effective measures like improving the storage facilities of food grains, so that wastage food grains can be avoided, prompt movement to places of need will go a long way in reducing food shortage to some extent. (T. Vijaya Raghavan, 2010).

If we want to achieve food sufficiency then we need to shift from subsidy and government sponsorship to people's participation approach.

What needs to be done? (IFPRI report, 2009)

- Need to distinguish food production and access to food as two different challenges
- In India at present access is a bigger issue than production. India's Challenge: National food surplus vs. local food insecurity (due to inter-state migration, rural–urban migration, PDS-related issues, etc.). Infrastructure challenges such as insufficient storage capacity for India's large stocks deepen the problem
- Climate change may make production more problematic in future

- There is some scope for increasing productivity, but it needs stronger incentives and better coordinated government programmes
- Risk insurance can also boost production
- Technology innovations for rain-fed area development and watershed development to enhance production are limited and need to be scaled up
- There is an urgent need to optimize land use
- Genetically Modified crops could boost production, but face strong reluctance because of misgivings in India. But there are some advocates and there is scope for wider dialogue with policy and programme makers
- Need for dialogue on India's trade restrictions and their impact on global/regional food security

Recommendations

- Need to create more evidence on the likely impact of climate change on food production/security
- Need for policy dialogue to revisit food and agriculture policies and ensure better incentives for production
- Assist through dialogue to make the PDS universal (self- targeting) and include more local foods in the PDS system in India
- Help India to emerge as a global player to boost regional/global food security (dialogue for lifting trade restrictions etc.)

References

1. Amartya Sen and Jean Dreze.
2. Bordignon, 2007.
3. Dr. R.S. Paroda, a former Director-General of the Indian Council of Agricultural Research (ICAR).
4. Dr. Lux Lakshmanan, Director, California Agriculture Consulting Service, Davis, California.
5. IFPRI report, 2009.
6. T. Vijaya Raghavan, 2010.

Chapter – 12

Tribal and their Environment

In India, the majority of the tribal population depends on forests and forest land for their survival and livelihood. This case study will enlighten you about the **Tribal and their Environment** conservation methods that they are using since time immemorial. The data was collected by me during great insurgency of 1987 in north east area. I wish to bring to your knowledge a case study of interaction between forest and tribal (forest dwellers) of Manipur-called HMARS. The largest concentration of HMAR found in Churachandpur, Tipaimukh and Jiribam subdivisions of Manipur. Forest is the main store house: from this cornucopia comes golden grain, ripe corn, fruits and vegetables to the Hmar house. It provides them not only food grains but building materials such as thatch cane, bamboos etc. to construct beautiful houses on the rows of hills. The forest provides them immense scope for hunting and trapping wild animals. It also provides them large area for Jhooming i.e slash and burn cultivation. In addition to corn, fruits and vegetables they grow cotton in their Jhoom field and weave attractive cloths (PUON). They prepare well finished baskets for their daily use. The musical tunes that enchant the listeners coming from different types of musical instruments (KHUONGS) are made up of bamboos comes from forest. Not only economic sustenance but the entire journey of life from the womb to tomb is completed by these tribal in the lap of forest. In Manipur, about one lakh hectare area of hills is under Jhoom or swiddening cultivation, of which 60000 hectares are estimated to be under jhooming every year involving 55000 tribal families. As such every tribal family owns 1.2 hectares of Jhooming land. To conserve environment and biodiversity, the Jhoomias(Jhoom cultivators) maintains 3-5 years period of consecutive cropping and fallowing in a a jhoom cycle and also adopt mix cropping alongwith the rotation of crop to enrich the soil in the jhoom field. They clear the forest land for jhooming in such a fashion that the stumps are never uprooted thereby saving the land from soil erosion and becoming infertile.

Forest, conservation and protected area laws in India: In India, Ownership and utilization of forest resources were vested with local communities or traditional governance structures until the advent of the British. The administration of the natural resources and its forest wealth in India started in 1864 by the British followed by the Indian Forest Act of 1865, which was the first attempt at legislation. With this began the shift in ownership of forests from people to the State thereby leading to the beginning of the conflict between State and communities over protection and utilization of forests. The Indian Forest Act which came into being in 1927 brought in three significations legal entities into the forest policy – the specific interpretation and legal mechanisms in defining Reserved Forests, Village Forests and Protected Forests. The concept of protected forests takes roots in this Act, giving the State government the right to declare any forest lands or waste lands not declared as reserved forests, as protected forests and prohibit/restrict the rights of private persons on these lands. The other important section of the Act which has not been implemented is the creation of village forests assigning rights over certain reserved forests to any village-community.

The Wildlife Protection Act of 1972 is the other legal framework created for classifying certain areas as national parks and sanctuaries in order to conserve wildlife by restricting the entry of private or commercial interests. However, since the creation of this Act there have been situations where local communities' needs were curtailed causing man-animal conflict on one side, and private commercial lobbies trying to circumvent the Act in order to do mining, quarrying and other industrial activities. Many of these conflicts are also in the form of legal battles at the high court and Supreme Court levels. The Eco Development programmes in the national parks were initiated to enhance the Wildlife Protection Act and to reduce local community interference with the environment.

The Forest Conservation Act of 1980 was enacted to provide for the conservation of forests by checking the indiscriminate diversion of forest land for non forest purposes and the need for clearance from the central government for approval of diversion of forest lands. However, the 1988 National Forest Policy made a signification shift in forest policy by stating the need to consider local community interests for utilization of forest resources and for involvement of local communities in protection and regeneration of forests. To a large extent, forest laws in India have had the most serious impacts on tribal communities whose customary laws and practices have been worst affected and even the constitutional safeguards provided to them stand threatened by newer shifts in forest and other economic policies.

The government of India has found that its traditional methods of forestry and biodiversity conservation approach in the country have not had a very positive impact on the regeneration and protection of forests.

Over the decades it has given way to certain shifts in the policy and programme designs towards forestry where regeneration of forest cover is now being conceived by making local communities inclusive partners of protection and sharing of the benefits of forests around them. The other important aspect is the recognition of the diversity of biological resources in the country and communities' traditional livelihood and social practices of management and protection as significant not only in the cultural sense, but also in administrative, management as well as economic definitions. [1]

Tribal laws and constitutional safeguards for tribal people

India followed a policy of social protection towards the marginalized sections of the country, like the scheduled castes and the scheduled tribes. The majority of the Scheduled Tribal population lives in the hilly and forest areas and their basic sustenance and livelihood are dependent on the natural and forest resources around them. The 100 million tribal populations (8% of the total population of the country) are protected by the Fifth Schedule of the Indian Constitution through legal mechanisms of ownership over lands and resources in the areas earmarked as the Scheduled Areas. These areas are spread across 8 states in the country and have corresponding state laws to protect the tribal people as enshrined in the Fifth Schedule.

1. FIFTH SCHEDULE is the constitutional safeguard for the tribal people in India and deals with "Provisions as to the Administration and Control of Scheduled Areas and Scheduled Tribes". Fifth Schedule (Article 244(1) Part 2 (a) prohibit or restrict the transfer of land by or among members of the Scheduled Tribes in such area; (b) regulate the allotment of land to members of the Scheduled Tribes in such area.

2. PESA The second most significant legislative protection for the tribal people in support of the Fifth Schedule is the enactment of the 73rd Amendment Act (Act. No.40) of 1996 which is known as the Panchayat

(Extension to Scheduled Areas) Act and came to be adopted in most of the states with scheduled areas, with corresponding laws. The Act clearly states the supremacy of the Gram Sabha (the decentralized unit of governance in the tribal areas) in the Scheduled Areas and right to self rule and governance of the tribal people. It empowers the Gram Sabhas to have control over resources and the right to "customary law, social and religious practices and traditional management practices of community resources."

Although the PESA Act 1996 prohibits the State Governments to make any law which is inconsistent with the provisions given in section 4, it has been noticed that the PESA enactments made by the State Governments vary from State to State and do not strictly correspond with the provisions of PESA Act.

3. Protected areas and natural resource laws in India

- According to section 18 of Wildlife (Protection) Act, 1972 the State Government may by notification declare any area as a sanctuary.
- According to section 32 of The India Forest Act, 1927 the State Government may make rules in Matters relating to the forest produce, grant licenses to inhabitants regarding use of forest produce and felling or removing trees and timber and the protection and management of any portion of a forest closed under section 30.
- Collection of any forest produce without the permission of the forest department in protected areas is a punishable offence.
- Fishing and Hunting in the Protected Animals is strictly prohibited.
- Movement of people is also very restricted in Protected Animals.

Through this law the Government initiated actions against tribal living in the forests which has been termed as **Historical Injustice to the tribal.**

The Government in 2004 decided to bring about legislation to recognize e forest and vest the forest rights and occupation in the forest land for these forest dwelling groups. **Thus, came into existence "The Schedule Tribes and other Traditional Forest Dwellers (Recognition of Forest Rights) Act, 2006".** The ST or tribal communities or other traditional forest dwellers, who had occupied forest lands before 13th, December 2005, are eligible for the rights.

State approach towards local communities with regard to forests and tribal people

The policing attitude ruled the system of governance which considered local forest dwelling communities as 'encroachers' and 'exploiters' of the forests. In many of the states which had tribal populations, there were revolts and resistance against these highhanded State laws. Tribal uprisings which were reckoned as part of the freedom movement in India are in reality, struggles against the oppressive forest regulations of the British and its exploitation of local communities in order to plunder these forest resources.

This oppressive attitude continued post independence where the State was considered the supreme authority over the forests and the local communities were regarded as exploiters of the forests. Besides, the nature of development pursued by the State led to large-scale displacement of forest dwelling communities and submergence of vast areas of forests for big development projects. Industries were given priority of access to forest resources or of destruction of forest cover, at highly subsidized costs whereas the same was denied to local villages. Notification of forests took place without proper consultation with the people and without recognition of their customary habitations and resource use within the forest areas.

Settlement of rights of forest dwelling communities was conducted in a highly lackadaisical manner leading to harassment of people by the forest officials. With the increase in paper, timber, mining and other industries in the forest areas bringing in new populations, the pressure on the local communities and on the natural resources multiplied spreading a vicious web of exploitation of the resources and of innocent tribal communities traditionally living in these regions.

The realization of the need for dialoguing with the local communities began when government failed to stop the large-scale deforestation which was caused both by people, large development projects and by industries. The alarming rate at which thousands of hectares of forests and biodiversity have become extinct, has led to the administration's focus on restrategising its intervention in forest conservation.

Social forestry programmes were initiated which in the 90's took the shape of joint forest management programmes under the influence of both internal rethinking and external financial institutions.

Quasi legal institutions and programmes like the Joint/Community Forest Management (J/CFM)

Programmes for forestry are being created currently in various states for conserving forests with huge external aid, also bringing in policy changes. At the national level there are contradictory processes happening in the forestry management approaches. On the one hand, there is a great impetus to participatory models of forest governance like the JFM programmes and on the other, there is an increasing pressure on local forest dwelling communities by the State by terming them as 'encroachers' and 'illegal' inhabitants of the forest regions, the greater pressure being on the tribal people whose existence in these regions for centuries is not being recognized.

A case of Palamau Tiger Reserve, Jharkhand

Palamau tiger reserve is located in the district of Palamau in Jharkhand. The area falls in what is known as the Chotanagpur plateau. The total area of the PA is 1026 sq. km and there are two divisions, namely, the Project Tiger Division and the Daltonganj South Forest division. Over 970 sq km area of Palamau Tiger Reserve was declared as Palamau Wildlife sanctuary in 1979. Out of this, an area of 226.32 sq km was notified as Betla National Park in 1996. Around 29 sq km is designated as a tourism zone.

There are three tribal villages, Ramandag, Latoo and Kujrum, in the core area of the park. The human and cattle populations in these villages are 549 and 643 respectively. These people belong to the tribes of Oraon, Kherwar, Korwa, Munda and Birjia tribes. Of the communities in the project affected area, 56% belong to the Scheduled Tribe and 15% to Scheduled Castes. There are 72 villages in the buffer zone of the Reserve and an additional 113 around it within a radius of 5 km. The total human population in these villages has been projected at over 116,550 out of which 39,000 people are living within the Reserve boundary. The project area is by and large free from encroachment.

The area faces severe drought almost every five years. There is a proposal to start underground coal mining near Horilong, about 1.6 km. from the Reserve boundary. This proposal is under consideration by the Central Government.

The Kutku Dam of the North Koel Multipurpose Hydroelectric Project, which would flood 15 villages (of which five are within the Reserve) could indirectly threaten Palamau Tiger Reserve. If the dam is ever made operational, people living in the submergence zone may be obliged to enter the forest area of the Reserve because the Water Resources Department has not yet complied with the stipulation laid down by the Government of India under the Forest Conservation Act, 1980, regarding rehabilitation of the villagers. It is, therefore, necessary that the people affected due to the proposed submergence are relocated suitably and no relocation takes place without their free prior and informed consent.

Tiger Reserve and Tribal forest villages

As reported by RR Prasad, there were 10 forest villages in 1993 in Palamu district which fall in the Daltonganj south forest division and Palamu Tiger Reserve. Due to creation of Tiger Reserve, certain restrictions were imposed on the local people residing near the core and buffer areas. The core area was closed for grazing cattle and cattle camps established in it were removed. Also felling of timber, cutting of bamboos and harvesting of minor forest produce were completely stopped. From the buffer area also the cattle camps were removed and restrictions were imposed on free will grazing, exploitation of timber was also stopped in the entire buffer area. Prior to the creation of Tiger Reserve, its forest were open to grazing, cattle camps etc. (Prasad 1993, pp47).

The tribal people living in forest villages do not get any development aid from the government since their villages not declared as revenue villages. Presently these villages are not having wells for drinking water, ponds, electricity, communication and transport facilities. (Prasad 1993, pp. 55).

In Palamu district, certain glaring irregularities have been committed in issuing land "PATTAS" to the forest villagers on the pretext that they fall under core area and have not been declared revenue villages and are to be relocated.

Bare facts- especially regarding the current situation of fauna of PTR are:

1. The Reserve is in absolute ruins with the authorities having absolutely no control over roughly 60 % of the reserve for more than 5 years now, having partial control (i.e. parts of the reserve where even though officers don't dare to go but the trackers and forest staff can manage to go in if forced to do so) over 30-35% and having complete control over just 5% of the Reserve (this includes two compartments of the Betla National Park)
2. The Forest is more or less still intact even though profitable trees that were abundant in our time (like Khair,Teak,etc.) have completely disappeared. These trees were used by Naxals for financing their insurgency.

3. Majority of the ungulate population now survives primarily in the few compartments of Betla National Park (core of PTR) and they have been all but wiped out from the rest of the Reserve.
4. The Elephant population has increased even though the already meager Tusker population has been further depleted.
5. Dholes mysteriously disappeared from Betla National Park(we were used to seeing healthy packs of Dholes in Betla and in Kujurum Forests in the interior of PTR) in 2002.There other prime habitat in Kujurum Forests has been out of the control of the authorities for more than 5 years and there hasn't been any assessment of the population that used to exist there. Reports from the villagers that live there indicate that they have vanished from Kujurum too. A few stragglers might have survived but in all likelihood dholes mysteriously went extinct from the Palamau tiger reserve somewhere around 2002-2003. The amazing part is that no inquiry has been carried out into their disappearance and this is because the officers don't even know that dholes were distributed in PTR and that they have gone extinct.
6. The Indian Bison or Gaur is also showing a decreasing trend and without remedial action, will go extinct in the near future as it has been wiped out from most of its former ranges in PTR. The bulk of the population survives in Betla and a few individuals are reported by locals from Kujurum Range.
7. One of the most wildlife rich ranges of PTR—Kujurum Range-which used to be a prime habitat of Sambar, Bisons, Dhole, Bear, Elephants, Leopards and Tigers apart from its other lesser denizens has been completely destroyed due to the insurgency. This range has been out of authoritative control for about 8 years. Most of its wildlife has been wiped off.
8. The forest rest house in Kujrum was also blasted and burned down by Naxals on the same day as the Kusumi Tree House in Maromar i.e. on 21st Aug 2007. Today the place has become almost inaccessible and the dilapidated roads are full of landmines. The staff(even the local trackers) doesn't dare to enter Kujurum. So one of the most important forests of PTR has been emptied of its great fauna.
9. The status of Wolves in unknown as the Mahuadanr Wolf Sanctuary (managed by PTR administration) as it hasn't been visited for a decade and the sanctuary is entirely in Naxal control. Other fauna

of the Reserve primarily survives in the Betla region with other areas of the reserve having almost all its fauna annihilated. (Kazmi 2010).

Conclusion:

In Manipur, about one lakh hectare area of hills is under Jhoom or swiddening cultivation, of which 60000 hectares are estimated to be under jhooming every year involving 55000 tribal families. As such every tribal family owns 1.2 hectares of Jhooming land. To conserve environment and biodiversity, the Jhoomias (Jhoom cultivators) maintains 3-5 years period of consecutive cropping and fallowing in a a jhoom cycle and also adopt mix cropping alongwith the rotation of crop to enrich the soil in the jhoom field. They clear the forest land for jhooming in such a fashion that the stumps are never uprooted thereby saving the land from soil erosion and becoming infertile.

The largest concentration of Hmar Tribe is found today in Churachandpur, Tipaimukh and Jibam sub-divisions of Manipur, North cachar hills of Assam, Meghalay, Mizoram and Tripura. Not only economic sustenance but the entire journey of life from the craddle to the graveyard is completed by the Hmar people in the lap of forest. Jhooming (Swiddening) Cultivation is the backbone of their economy. Their traditional Style and the indigenous, Environmental and Technical Knowledge for Jhooming have allowed them to survive all the dangers living in the forest (Sharma, 1992).

The Study of facts speaks itself that the Jhooming never endanger the Environment hence falsify the popular belief about environmental Pollution by Jhooming. Forest is the life line for tribal so, how can we say that tribal life style is against forest/ environment conservation? How can we say the tribal are posing dangers to environment?

To conclude, the myth that 'tribal and their culture is against modern biodiversity conservation principle and law" has no logical basis. Tribal forest and biodiversities in the area survived together for centuries.

References

Devullu.P.et al, 2004,Indigenous and tribal communities, biodiversity conservation and the Global Environment Facility in India, SAMTA, Hyderabad.

Prasad. R.R et al 1993 Tribal situation in Forest Villages-Changing subsistence strategy and adaptation, Discovery Publishing House, New Delhi.

Kazmi. Raja 2010 A MELANCHOLIC HOME COMING : Return to Palamau Tiger Reserve(PTR)—The Heartland of Wildlife and Naxalism in Jharkhand, internet blog on Sanctuary.

The Indian Forest Act, 1927 [Act No. 16 of 1927].

The Wild Life (Protection) Act, 1972 [No. 53 of 1972].

Sharma. V.P, 1992 The Hmars of Manipur: An Anthropological Exploration; Anmol Publications, New Delhi.

Chapter – 13

Globalization and its Effect in General and on Tribal in Particular

The largest concentrations of Tribal peoples are found in the seven states of north-east India, and the so-called "central tribal belt" stretching from Rajasthan to West Bengal. India has several laws and constitutional provisions, such as the Fifth Schedule for mainland India and the Sixth Schedule for certain areas of north-east India, which recognize indigenous peoples' rights to land and self-governance. The critics of globalization typically emphasize that globalization is a process that is mediated according to corporate interests, and typically raise the possibility of alternative global institutions and policies, which they believe address the moral claims of poor and working classes throughout the globe, as well as environmental concerns in a more equitable way. It seems to be true in case of Indigenous people of Jharkhand as the laws aimed at protecting indigenous peoples have numerous shortcomings and their implementation is far from satisfactory. India has a long history of indigenous peoples' movements aimed at asserting their rights.

Tribal peoples are the holders of unique languages, knowledge systems and beliefs and possess invaluable knowledge of practices for the sustainable management of natural resources. They have a special relation to and use of their traditional land. Their ancestral land has a fundamental importance for their collective physical and cultural survival as peoples. Indigenous peoples hold their own diverse concepts of development, based on their traditional values, visions, needs and priorities.

Legal rights and policy developments

The laws aimed at protecting tribal peoples have numerous shortcomings and their implementation is far from satisfactory. India has a long history of indigenous peoples' movements aimed at asserting their rights.

On 25 November 2010, the Ministry of Tribal Affairs requested that the Prime Minister of India issue suitable instructions for obtaining clearance from the Ministry of Tribal Affairs for a "Rehabilitation and Resettlement Plan" for all the development projects which involve displacement of tribal communities. However, the Ministry received no response from the Prime Minister to this proposal.

On 3 September 2010, an 18-member National Council for Tribal Welfare, headed by the Prime Minister of India, was constituted to provide broad policy guidelines for the implementation and monitoring of welfare schemes for tribals. It is also supposed to review the implementation of the Forest Rights Act, and monitor the implementation of the Tribal Sub-Plan and programmes aimed at protecting vulnerable tribal groups. The National Council for Tribal Welfare comprises Union Ministers for Tribal Affairs, Finance, Home, Agriculture, Health and Family Welfare, Environment and Forests, Human Resource Development, Rural Development, Woman and Child Development, Culture, Mines and Coal, and Power, the Deputy Chairperson of the Planning Commission and Chief Ministers of concerned states, among others.

In India, 461 ethnic groups are recognized as Scheduled Tribes, and these are considered to be India's indigenous peoples who are otherwise referred as the Scheduled Tribes or Adivasis, which literally means indigenous peoples. With an estimated population of 84.3 million, they comprise 8.2% of the total population. There are, however, many more ethnic groups that would qualify for Scheduled Tribe status but which are not officially recognized. Estimates of the total number of tribal groups are as high as 635.

In Jharkhand, there are 32 scheduled tribes with different racial types, speaking different dialects of various linguistic affinities as given in the table next page.

	Name	*Habitation : of Tribes*	*Racial Types Districts of*	*Dialect*	*Linguistic*	*Remarks Affinity*
1.	Asur	Gumla, Lohardaga Palamou, Latehar	Proto Australoid	Asuri	Austro -Asiatic	
2.	Baiga	Highlands of central India	Proto Australoid	Sadani	Indo-Aryan	
3.	Banjara	Raj mahal ,Godda, Santhal pargana	Proto Australoid	Sadani	Indo-Aryan	
4.	Bathudi	Singhbhum	Proto Australoid	Mixed	Indo-Aryan	
5.	Bedia	Ranchi, Hazaribag, Singhbhum, Santhal pargana	Proto Australoid	Sadani	Indo-Aryan	
6.	Binjhia	Simdega, Khunti,	Proto Australoid	Sadani	Indo-Aryan	
7.	Birhor	Dhanbad, Gumla, Giridh, Garhwa, Hazaribag, Lohardaga, Palamu, Ranchi	Proto Australoid	A dialect of Mundari	Austro-Asiatic	
8.	Birjia	Gumla, Lohardaga, Palamu, Ranchi	Proto Australoid	Sedan, Bengali	Indo-Aryan	
9.	Bhumij	Gumla, Lohardaga, Singhbhum, Ranchi, Hazaribagh, Dhanbad	Proto Australoid	A dialect of Mundar, Sadani and Bengali	Austro-Asiatic / Indo-Aryan	
10.	Chero	Palamu ,Latehar, Ranchi, Santhal pargana l	Proto Australoid	Mundari	Austro-Asiatic	No language of its own
11.	Chick-Baraik	Gumla, Lohardaga, Ranchi	Proto Australoid	Sadani	Indo-Aryan	
12.	Gond	Ranchi, Palamu, Singhbhum	Proto Australoid	Gondi	Dravidian	
13.	Gorait	Hazaribag, dhanbad, singhbhum Lohardaga, Palamu, Ranchi, Santhal pargana	Proto Australoid	Sadani	Indo-Aryan	
14.	Ho	Singhbhum	Proto Australoid	Ho	Austro-Asiatic	
15.	Karmali	Hazaribag, Bokaro, Singhbhum, Ranchi, Santhal pargana	Proto Australoid	Karmali	Austro-Asiatic	
16.	Kharia	Gumla, Ranchi,Singhbhum, Hazaribagh	Proto Australoid	Kharia	Austro-Asiatic	
17.	Kharwar	Chatra, Garhwa, Hazaribag, Latehar Lohardaga,Palamu, Ranchi	Proto Australoid	Sadani	Indo-Aryan	
18.	Khond	Singhbhum, Hazaribagh	Proto Australoid	Khond	Austro-Asiatic	
19.	Kisan	Hazaribag, Dhanbad, Singhbhum, Ranchi, Santhal pargana,Garhwa, Hazaribag, Latehar Lohardaga, Palamu, Ranchi	Proto Australoid	Mundari	Austro-Asiatic	No language of its own
20.	Kora	Dumka, Godda, Deoghar, Pakur, Banka, Sahebganj, Dhanbad, Bokaro, Hazaribagh, Chaibasa	Proto Australoid	A dialect of Mundari	Austro-Asiatic	

(Contd...)

21.	Korwa	Hazaribag, Dhanbad, Ranchi, Santhal pargana, Latehar, Palamu,	Proto Australoid	Korwa	Austro-Asiatic	Closely related to Asuri
22.	Lohra	Hazaribag, Singhbhum, Ranchi, Santhal pargana, Palamu	Proto Australoid	Sadani	Indo-Aryan	
23.	Mahli	Hazaribag, Singhbhum, Ranchi, Santhal pargana, Gumla, Dhanbad	Proto Australoid	Mahle	Austro-Asiatic	Mahle is sub-dialect of Santali
24.	Mal-Paharia	Dumka, Jamtara, Deoghar, Godda	Proto Australoid	Malto	Dravidian	Now they speak Bengali Sadani Hindi
25.	Munda	Hazaribag, Singhbhum, Ranchi, Santhal pargana, Palamu, Gumla, Giridih	Proto Australoid	Mundari	Austro-Asiatic	
26.	Oraon	Hazaribag, Singhbhum, Ranchi, Santhal pargana, Palamu, Garhwa, Dhanbad, Latehar. Lohardaga, Gumla	Proto Australoid	Kurukh	Dravidian	
27.	Parahia	Ranchi, Gumla, Hazaribagh, Santhal pargana, Palamu	Proto Australoid	Sadani	Indo-Aryan	
28.	Santhal	Hazaribag, Singhbhum, Ranchi, Santhal pargana, Giridih, Dhanbad,	Proto Australoid	Santhali	Austro-Asiatic	
29.	Sauria Paharia	Godda, Pakur, Rajmahal	Proto Australoid	Malto	Dravidian	
30.	Savar	Singhbhum	Proto Australoid	Kharia	Austro-Asiatic	Hill-Kharias are called Savars
31.	Kol	Dumka, Deoghar, (Included Giridih in ST category in 2003)	Proto Australoid	Kol	Austro-Asiatic	Similar to Santhali
32.	Kawar	Palamu, Gumla, (Included Simdega in ST category in 2003)	Proto Australoid	Sadani	Indo-Aryan	

Sources: Land and People of Jharkhand, JTWRI, Ranchi, 2003;Land and People of Tribal Bihar, BTRI, Ranchi, 1961.

Discussion

India has several laws and constitutional provisions, such as the Fifth Schedule for mainland India and the Sixth Schedule for certain areas of north-east India, which recognize tribal not indigenous peoples' rights to land and self-governance.

In the globalization process the Indian tribals are prone to exploitation and have been making vulnerable, the efforts have to be made so that vulnerability would be stopped.

Besides the processes of social change like westernization, modernizations, there is an impact of globalization by disarticulating and disturbing the tribal social institutions, the efforts of the globalization are to be directed towards the institution building, social or cohesive bondage, institutional mechanism, value system- based in the tribal social system.

Globalization has been impacting the tribals' subsistence economy in the name of income generation. The international financing system such as World Bank, IMF and the other donor agencies are funding the major or mega projects in the name of sustainable development, which has far reaching results, in the end of day project will be withdrawn leaving the tribal on the verge of destroyed economy. Instead the projects are to be designed in the tribal lands for reducing poverty by producing quality forest and tribal products on bio-resources and bio-diversities based, making value added and to get the market linkages.

Due to construction of large-scale irrigation projects, infrastructural establishments, industrial complexes, disruption, displacement and migration of large number of peoples in these mega projects have been taken place. Those affected people are neither compensated nor resettled properly. So rehabilitation-cum- resettlement policies have to be implemented as policy objectives and decisions, specially focussing on indigenous integrated farms and exploring of the perception of the tribal peoples.

The globalization is to be associated with combating climate change with the introduction of the sustainable and clean technologies to attempt the 'go- zero and zero-emission' with the reduced carbon emissions for ecological sustainability.

The promotion of the indigenous knowledge specially indigenous technologies is to be made for the community well being linking electronic technology after the research and development on bench-marking for the local market gaining.

In the information and communication technologies e-governance is to be strengthened to disseminate the information of the development opportunities and the identification of the problems and issues.

The globalization requires electricity for production and daily consumption due to up-gradation of the life standards. More emphasis is to be given for producing non-conventional alternative energies like solar, wind or hydro-electricity by providing with electricity and supplying the energy giving materials by cultivating the bio-fuels.

The tourism sector has to be developed with development of nature tourism, rural tourism and eco-tourism for bio-diversity management, community livelihood development and imparting environmental education.

Ethno-eco tourism site is to be established with the promotion of ethnic foods, ethno-medicines or ethnic dresses in the indigenous lands.

The foreign direct investment is to be made towards afforestation and reforestation for the development of livelihoods and income-flow and also mitigating the carbon emission.

The utility of mobile phones are to be made by providing the information of the job market and product market.

Micro-finance has to be developed to develop small and micro-enterprise development.

Globalization is world-wide drive for domination of the corporation or corporate sector, which is to be mobilized towards accountability in the democratic process with more development of corporate social responsibilities.

The human capital development in the tribal areas. is to be strengthened by giving quality education or knowledge management in the ICT sector and also professional management system.

There is large impact of industrialization of modern pharm industries on the tribal health. Health care measures are to be taken by introducing of ethno-medicine and follow up health tourism based making in association with culture and traditions on the natural products . Some diseases like HIV/AID are found prevalent in the tribal belt as the impact of globalization, which should be removed by developing the awareness.

Shift from manufacturing to the service sector encourages weakening at the labour unions and exploiting people in the labour wages.

In the globalization process tribals are subjected to capitalistic exploitation as large section of the tribal population work as unskilled workers and they are forced into low paid labour sections.Union Government Or state govts. in India, should ensure through policy and legislations that minimum harm would be taken place as tribals are at the mercy of the employers.

The processes of globalization are to be made on the theme- 'Think globally and act locally'. So at the local level the civil societies are to be formed into self-help groups at the village levels and subsequent federations from block to the divisions or districts for the entrepreneurial activities and for the community empowerment.

Examining the Impact of "Globalisation on Tribals in India", B. Ezhilarasu,(Economics, Vol. 4, 2014) attracted attention with following observations. "The new economic policies have serious impact on the adivasi lives whose right over access to natural resources, livelihood opportunities, right to primary education and health, protection from atrocities and human rights abuses and the right to uphold their traditional and customary practices, are under series threat due to the changes in laws and policies. The most serious threat to the adivasi people on the country today is the pressure on the Fifth Schedule. Both Central and Several state governments are seriously making efforts to amend the laws prescribed under Fifth Schedule and their corresponding state laws in order to allow private and corporate players to take over tribal and forest lands. Violation of the Fifth Schedule has occurred in many states like in Andhra Pradesh where the Land Transfer Regulation Act was ignored while giving mining leases in scheduled areas to private companies. The new Industrial policy paved the way for Tribal Land alienation. These results in the alienation of tribal lands for various purpose like construction dams, mining projects, setting up of wildlife sanctuaries, construction of government infrastructure and encroachments by non tribals. While the adivasis have been displaced and pushed into the fringes of globalization, the natural resources were victim to large scale destruction directly for industry purposes and indirectly by the non tribals. As a result the tribals ended up as debris in the globalised policies unable to access the resources which were their life sustaining forces or to compete with the mainstream society to be absorbed into alternate economies. Those absorbed in the new industries and projects were minimal compared to the extent of displacement and the destruction of traditional livelihood. Globalisation may also weaken the constitutional protections, in terms of education and job reservations given to tribals. Hence the Government should frame Special policy and programmes that are required to address the issue". (B. Ezhilarasu 2014, Economics, Vol. 4)

The critics of globalization typically emphasize that globalization is a process that is mediated according to corporate interests, and typically raise the possibility of alternative global institutions and policies, which they believe address the moral claims of poor and working classes throughout the globe, as well as environmental concerns in a more equitable way. It seems to be true in case of tribal of Jharkhand as the laws aimed at protecting

Tribal peoples have numerous shortcomings and their implementation is far from satisfactory.

References

Fact Sheet, UN permanent Forum on Indigenous Issues.United Nations.

The Indigenous World 201.1,Edited by: Kathrin Wessendorf Pages: 548,ISSN: 1024-0217, ISBN: 978-87-91563-97-3, May 2011.

Land and People of Jharkhand, JTWRI, Ranchi, 2003.

Land and People of Tribal Bihar, BTRI, Ranchi, 1961.

Chapter – 14

From hill to plain: An Experiment in Applied and Action Anthropology in India

Even after sixty years of independence, our tribal brethren are facing enormous problems in maintaining their livelihood as well as ethnic identity. There has been considerable fund allocation through all the 11 five years' plans of Government of India for development of these groups but the ground reality indicates towards their grim situation.

PAHARI - KORWA and *Birhor* are two primitive tribal groups inhabiting larger area of the hills of the district. There have been good efforts for their development by Jashpur administration but it is felt that they require urgent inputs from the academia about their eco-cultural situation for better implementation of development programmes.

Though there were many anthropological studies conducted in the past about their life and culture as scholarly exercises but the regional variations in cultural pattern could not attract attention. Thus, the development plans made on the generalized findings were of little help.

According to Vidyarthi (1978), "the scope of research in the field of applied research in India is very wide especially when the whole traditional society is in the process of large scale transformation. In proportion to the magnitude of the task, the output to the applied social anthropologists and sociologists has not been adequate. Though, role of the social anthropologists and other behavioural scientists in the various fields of national reconstruction is acknowledged, their impact and contributions have not been as desired. There are many reasons for such a situation of applied social sciences in this country. The role of social anthropologists has not been well defined in the bureaucratic machinery of the State and Central Governments. There is no unanimity even among the anthropologists themselves regarding their roles as analysts, advisers, and co-operators. It seems that the applied social scientists in India should gracefully accept the various roles suggested above if certain conditions are satisfied. Firstly, he should have appropriate status in organisational setup, and secondly, once a subject for investigation is agreed upon through consultation, he must be free to draw up design and the tools of investigations, and thirdly, he must be able to present his findings at the highest policy level."

Writing on categories of applied anthropologists in India Vidyarthi (1978, 176-177) clarify five types such as:

I. Those who act as consultants on the staff of administration and usually function under the control of the administrators.

II. The second types are those who are consultants primarily to the administrators but are outsiders i.e. they are not on the regular pay roll of the organisation.

III. The researcher and administrator work together as co-administrators.

IV. A social anthropologist is at least temporarily in actual charge of the development programme of a community which he and his associates are studying.

V. The fifth category is represented by action anthropology of Sol Tax which can function only in an independent manner and in institutions where an action anthropologist can combine both action and research.

Elucidating the above in Indian context, Vidyarthi mentioned that there are several anthropologists in the first thee categories but the fourth is represented only by two cases in India, First, in Tamia Block by B.H. Mehta, who has combined research and development under the auspices of Gondwana Research and Development Centre. The second by P.K. Bhowmik, who successfully combined the two processes of "helping and learning" among an ex-criminal tribe the Lodhas of West Bengal. The fifth category remained unrepresented in India although L.P. Vidyarthi initiated one Action anthropology programme at Neterhat Pat Region of Jharkhand but remained unfinished.

This paper presents the case study of a successful effort in the fifth category to bridge the gap between knowledge and practice that is the felt need of the hour to have a clear understanding of contemporary situation of the above mentioned primitive tribal groups in ecological setting of Jashpur District of Chattishgarh for better planning and implementation of need based development programmes by the district authorities.

It was proposed in 1997 that an Applied and Action Anthropology programme be commissioned urgently to study contemporary life and culture of these people with special emphasis on their ecology and problems and to implement some kind of development project to better their lives.

Dr. V.P.Sharma, Senior Anthropologist from G.G. University, Bilaspur started Applied and Action Anthropology intervention programme among *PAHARI KORWA* of Bagicha and Manora block in 1997 in collaboration with Tribal and Rural Development Institute of Jashpurnagar, Madhya Pradesh now Chhatishgarh.

Applied and Action Anthropological intervention

While metropolitan India is moving along a different tangent, her valleys, ghatis and impenetrable forests provide refuse to cultures which retain elements of great antiquity. These are her adivasies- a people with a remote past but no recorded history. If you want to search for the thread of life pattern of another age, take a journey to Jashpur in Chattisgarh, where the hinterland has made pursuit of the wildest tribe- the *PAHARI KORWA*- impossible.

Scholars like Dalton (1872), Majumdar (1847), and Vidyarthi(1958) have called them 'Primitive'. These tribes are comparatively backward in all spheres of life. Every aspects of their life possess a problem. Illiteracy, Simple economy, lowest standard of production and consumption, Semi nakedness, exploitation are their several complex problems.

This is how Colonel Dalton, a colonial surveyor of the Ethnology of Bengal fame, records his tryst with them more than a century ago:

> *"They are the most savage and terrifying in appearance, but have good humouredly accepted the following singular tradition to account for it: they believe that the first human beings that settled in Sarguja, being very much troubled by the degradations of wild beasts on their crops, put up scarecrows in their fields."*

Most of the studies on Pahari Korwa tribes are anthropological and sociological and deals with their origin, social and cultural aspects, only a few studies have been conducted on the economic development of the

Pahari Korwa. Studies on impact of local eco-system of the Pahari Korwa are scant.

This study is an attempt in this direction to study the impact of economic development programme and local eco-system on the socio-cultural values and economy of the Pahari Korwa tribe and to see the socio-economic characteristics of Pahari Korwa and the role of the development programme in shaping and building their subsistence economy.

The Pahari Korwa appear to have occupied the minds of rulers and administrators for the last hundred and ten years. The earliest account of the Pahari Korwa has been given by Dalton (1969). Others who have furnished information on the Korwa are Risley and Gait (1901), De Breh (1909), Hutton (1946), Crooks (1892), Bhaduri (1937), Majumdar (1930), Singh (1957) Prasad and Bhandari (1961,1963), Ahmad (1973), Sandhawar (1973), Mishra & Mishra (1998).

Dalton (1872) feels that the Korwa were the first habitants of the area and were the one time master of the savage and almost nomadic. They were at one time more numerous and powerful and it is possible that many of the broken tribes now found scattered through out this part of India once formed with the Korwa people united under some rude form of government.

Risely and Gait (1901) in the census of India, furnish the following information regarding the Korwa and distribution of their population in central India. The only consideration of the tribe of western Bengal who speaks Munda language are the Korwa and who appears to be related to Munda, inhabit the west of Chotanagpur especialy the state of Surguja and Jashpur. Here their language is called Korwai (Korwari).

De Breh (1909) in the beginning of twentieth century depicts the Korwa in the following words:

> "The Korwa are liable to outbreaks of crime, which usually takes the form of an attack on the Ahir, a class of man, who by their reckless manner in which they allow their cattle to damage the cultivation of these aborigines, often excite the latter to reprisals, occasionally they also attack the passing traders to get salt or cloth, or a liquor shop to get a supply of drink. These men are usually armed with bows and arrows, spears and axes and since they do not hesitate to use their weapons and are usually in considerable force, they are formidable opponents to unarmed people"

Risley, Hutton, Crooks, Driver, Russell and Hiralal and Prasad have made only passing reference to Hill Korwa. Thus their accounts shed little light on the life and culture of the people.

Majumdar, conducted field work among the Korwa of Mirzapur (UP), Surguja and Palamau. Bhandari has studied kinship organization of the Korwa of Mirzapur (UP) only. Prasad's brief account of the people is based on the Korwa of Palamau (Jharkhand) and Singh has made a brief mention of Korwa while bringing in to relief the past and present of the Surguja district Ahmad has only dwelt upon the physical aspect of the hill Korwa of Surguja, Sandhwar discusses the impact of Christian missionaries on the Korwa of Palamau.

The first ever empirical literature on Pahari Korwa was produced by Waltyre in 1844, Rorings "Hindu castes and tribes "(1972). In this present Changing period various census reports and related ethnographic notes are the sources of literature on tribes Central Provinces census report (1881) and 1891 Census of India (1911), (1921) and their community wise Characteristics social life and religion wise information on Pahari Korwa are included. In this colonel ward (1889), V.Robertsan (1893), W.H. Stuarts "The Korwa census of India 1933 are some of the very important literature on Pahari Korwa and are particularly important as far as the social life and anthropological characteristic are concerned. Guha B.S (1935) gave description about Pahari Korwa's anthropological feature social and economic activities and also included religious beliefs. In this series of Pahari Korwa literature contribution of Russell & Hiralal (1916) is always remembered as one of the initial literary work on the tribes which at that period of time summed up much information on the castes and tribes including Pahari Korwa of the Central India. This study was empowered by having folk stories & songs and various anthropological features, social and economic activities and religious & cultural beliefs that were available up to that point of time.

Russell and Hiralal have considered Korwa as the offshoot of Munda of Chotanagpur. Bhandari(1937) and Prasad (1961) have studied the presence of Pahari Korwa in Mirzapur in U.P. and Palamu in Bihar, Colonel Daltan(1960) believed that Korwa were the rulers of this entire province. Particularly due to nomadic and wild nature these couldn't increase at a larger scale. According to him Korwa are the sub-group of the Munda tribes of Chotanagpur plateau and these Munda tribe are as sub-families of the huge Asiatic family. Risley and Gait (1901) have also written in census of India that Korwa are basically the tribes of west Bengal who speak Munda language and there inhabiting area is the western part of Chotanagpur plateau i.e. Jashpur and Surguja. Here, there language is known as *Korwai* which is spoken like ingle language. In the beginning of 20th Century D.Brett (1989) had recognized that Pahari Korwa as one of the criminal & violent tribes who had regular violent clash with the people of Ahir caste. The main cause of this dispute was the grazing of cattle's belonging to the Ahirs in the Korwa agriculture land. Korwa used to attack on salt & cloth merchants passing through the jungle. They also attacked on local wine shops for wine Pahari Korwa were always powerfully dressed with bows & arrows and used them in normal conditions.

Risley, Hutton, Brooks Damien, Russell & Hiralal, has very briefly focused on the social and cultural life of the Pahari Korwa. W.V. Green sons and Barar (1944) have found that primitive tribes are facing accelerated reduction in land belongings. They gradually started loosing their land ownership and stepped down as owners of small land holdings.

None of the above mentioned studies have dealt with the socio-economic conditions of the Korwa with considerable depth. Dalton however has dealt with the Korwa life in general and brings in to relief some important fact about the origin of the people and distribution of their population in the last phase of the nineteenth Century A.D.

National council of applied economic research, New Delhi had conducted a survey on Socio-economic status of the primitive tribes of Madhya Pradesh and Published its report in the year 1963. On the primitive tribes of Madhya Pradesh other important data is available. In its important observation it was discovered that more than 80 per cent of the total income of an average primitive family is not in the form of currency as compared with the non-tribal area as this percentage is almost double in the tribal areas.

Bahadur (1966), in his study conducted on the Pahari Korwa had accepted the traditional importance of shifting cultivation but due to administrative control this practice had declined at a greater pace. Collection of forest products, roots, hunting, fishing and agricultural labour are the important activities of the Pahari Korwa. There habitat is mostly located in the hill far from the populated areas. The distance between the two Pahari Korwa families is more than 1-2 kms. Their main food is *Gondli, Mahua, Kutki*, rice and Pulse(*urad,kulthi,arhar*) roots, vegetables, fish and flesh of other animals. Their main drink is rice bear(*Handia)* made from rice.

D.N. Tiwari (1984), in one of his very important work has focused on the socio-economic position of Pahari Korwa. At present Pahari Korwa are also dependent on pre-agriculture level of technology and their local improvement also affect their activities. Pahari Korwa economy is dependent on forest. The destruction of forest has presented a circumstantial imbalance before this primitive tribe. The circumstances around them have not changed physically to greater extent.

The *PAHARI KORWA* is the least known, neglected and one of the Primitive Tribes of erstwhile Madhya Pradesh now Chhattisgarh. The neighboring tribal communities like Nagesia, Dehari (Plane) Korwa and Oraon call them as ***Vanala*** means one who lives in the forest.

PAHARI KORWA settled on hills and in dense forest, has numerical strength of 13486 (Survey, 1986; by PAHARI KORWA VIKASABHIKARAN, Jashpurnagar), in M.P. (now Chhattisgarh) Hill Korwas inhabit Raigarh, Surguja, and hill areas of Bilaspur district of Chhattisgarh in Bagicha Block their numerical strength is 4977(Census 1981, Adimjati Vikas Khand, Bagicha)**General profile of Programme Area:**

Jashpur is situated in the North-East part of Chhattisgarh, densely covered with green forest. The north part of the district is encircled with series of Forest Hills embedded with natural beauty. There are so many charming natural scenes in Bagicha, Manora, Jashpur and Kunkuri blocks, suited to be developed as tourist spots. The district incorporates rich tribes such as; Oroan, Nagwanshi, Gond and Kanwar as wel as most backward tribes like; Pahadi-Korwa and Birhor. Oroan dialect "Kurukh" is spoken in Oraon populated area while Sadari dialect is mostly spoken in the whole district.

The state high way connecting M.P. & Chhattisgarh with Jharkhand & Orissa, passes through this district. The district lacks in mass transportation system. The only means of transportation is private buses connecting it to M.P., Jharkhand, Orrissa, and state capital Raipur. Industrialization is far away from here being situated in remote hilly area. Gram Panchayats have tried to connect every village/hamlets with the main road by kaccha roads. It is essential to link the district with railway for speedy development.

Historical background

Jashpur is surrounded with Sarguja in the North-East, Raigarh district in the South-West, Orissa in the South-East and Jharkhand state in the East. District was inaugurated on May 25th 1998. Most part of the district is covered by hills and plateaus. On the basis of topography the district can be divided in two parts i.e. Upper-Ghat, the upper region and Neech-Ghat, lower region of the district.

Geographical Features

Jashpur district is situated in North-East of India between $22^0\,23^0\,0^0$ latitude and $83^0\,84^0\,0^0$ longitude. Area of the district is 6088 sq. km & situated at 771 meter high from the Mean Sea Level.

Natural Status

North region of the district is hilly and rocky containing Sandy soil on the small plains. There is no fertile land that's why mixed type of crop is grown here. Farmers grow Paddy, Oilseeds, and Pulses to meet their requirement. The land of Lower Ghat that is mostly plain and fertile in comparison with Upper GHAT. Irrigation facility is provided in lower GHAT by building stop dams across the small rivers. Farmers residing here grow Kharif as well as Rabi crops too. The main perennial rivers of the district are Lawa, Ib, Mainee and Shankh.

Climate

The climate of the district is peculiar. The upper part of the district is much colder whereas lower region is warm. The climate of the district is moist as heavy rain fall occurs here. Average Rain Fall = 1512.80 mm in the area.

Forest & Wildlife

Vast area i.e. 52.51% of the district is covered with dense forest and Sal is the predominant species. Sagwan saplings have been planted in some regions, which are growing well, but Sarai (Sal) is more suitable. The climate of this area is completely suitable for the Sal. Other species like Mango, Jack fruit, Black berry are also found here. Forest is rich in medicinal plants. Earlier different kinds of enormous wild animals were found here, but declining forest has reduced their number.

Process of intervention: The AAA Approach

Regular interaction resulted into confidence building. A Socio-Economic survey was carried out to know their problems and with the help of local government many developmental programmes were implemented by the Institute.

PRA exercises were conducted; training programmes were organized to bring these hill dwellers in the main stream of national life. A great

Tribal congregation of *PAHARI KORWA* was organized at Hrapat in 2000 where the institute developed the idea of bringing them on plains as plain settlers.

Regular interaction resulted into confidence building among most primitive tribal group *PAHARI KORWA* of Chhattishgarh. Counseling exercises were conducted; training programmes were organized to bring these hill dwellers in the main stream of national life by rehabilitating them on plains. A Tribal congregation of *PAHARI KORWA* was organized at Hrapat in 2000 where the institute developed the idea of bringing them on plains as plain settlers.

After long persuasion 13 families agreed to settle down on plains. The Institute convinced government to sanction PTG Housing scheme for them. Finally, thirteen families themselves volunteered to construct their own houses. A cherished dream of TRDI, under Applied and Action Anthropology Programme became reality in 2004.

Now, it was important to introduce livelihood development programme for these most primitive tribal group *PAHARI KORWA* of Chattishgarh. For this, the institute implemented an UNDP supported Technology Management Programme (TMP). Under this programme, the institute has established block level Technology Resource Center (TRC) for Jashpur block in collaboration with Regional Research Laboratory, Bhopal.

Technology, employment and tribal each one of these terms has baffled and divided both the academicians and the practitioners since long, especially during last few decades. (Sharma and Singh, 1988)

Gurnar Myrdal, commenting on employment policy, emphasized in his epic study about Asia that" If by a miracle, the cultivators in South Asia could be induced to work more diligently, Production would rise dramatically".

Technology has been widely acknowledged as a critical parameter in the production system. Generally speaking in a broader sense of the term, it has been identified practically with each and every aspect involved in the process of development or change, in fact technology represents in a way the unending human struggle for a better existence in his/her environment."

If employment is to be generated in a tribal region, it should be and can be best done by promoting and strengthening the existing modes of production of the people with the inputs of modern science and technology in a manner that the advantages of the existing system as well as those created by men to exploit the resources are combined." (quoted in Sharma and singh, 1988).

The basic idea behind the project was to promote the traditional occupation and to introduce people's friendly new rural technology, upgrading of their skills, provision of raw materials and modern equipments, credit support and marketing facility for the development of livelihood of rural and tribal people.

In specific terms, the project aimed at setting up a Common facility centre for training, demonstration and popularization of small scale industrial packages for identified cluster of 6 villages in Manora block.

To strengthen the existing units under initial stage and to introduce new technologies that is tested in other tribal areas, two institutions UNDP and IFAD were approached through Government of Madya Pradesh and Government of Chhattisgarh.

Tribal and Rural Development Institute adopted some villages under UNDP programme and introduced Mushroom production, Beekeeping, Beehive box manufacturing, Production of Herbal pesticides, production of fishing trap, Cultivation and storage of medicinal plants, wooden handicraft, MANDAR (beating drum) production, Bamboo basket production, Broom making and marketing, Leaf mat, leaf bowl and leaf plate production etc. were introduced in the Cluster of 25 tribal dominated villages in Manora block of Jaspur district.

In the second step, International Fund for Agricultural Development (IFAD) sanctioned watershed projects covering 6 villages for three years duration, Micro watershed code 4G2B6G - 1. Total geographical area of the Watershed was 1109.214 hectares out of which750.826 hectares were treatable area. There were 299 households inhabited by 1714 people (Male-884, Female-830).

The institute completed three years **Shaila watershed project** (2003-6) covering Six villages sanctioned by CGTDP, Government of Chhattisgarh, funded by International Fund for Agricultural Development (IFAD) and undertook following important activities:

1. 15 days training to 20 farmers on Fish Farming and Nylon net weaving.
2. Seven days training to 80 farmers on Bee –Keeping.
3. Two months training to two persons on Bee-box making skill.
4. Fifty two farmers were trained on Vermi-compost and construction of permanent pit.

5. Four farmers were trained in PAIRRA Treatment.
6. Three Anganwadi centres, one each in Shaila, Chattauri and Chirotoli village were constructed.
7. One EGS building was constructed at village Kardana.
8. Two water ponds were constructed at village Chattauri and are used for fisheries.
9. Sixteen Indira Awas for Primitive Tribal Group (Pahari Korwa) were constructed in village Chattauri. This is first ever novel attempt to inhabit hill dwellers on plane. The 16 Pahari Korwa families themselves contributed their labour in construction of their own houses. This is one of the most successful programme of the Institute.
10. Construction of 207 meters RRC village approach road at village Shaila using local M L A fund.
11. Under Goat Farming activity 45 goats were distributed to 14 Shelf Help Groups for pursuing sustained livelihood.
12. Construction of 14 Goat sheds in PTG colony of Chattauri village.
13. Building for Vocational Training centre was constructed at Village Chattauri.
14. Construction of one Stop –check- dam with canal at village Shaila.
15. Vegetable mini kits were distributed to 60 farmers.
16. 600 kgs Potato seeds were distributed among 34 members of BPL –SHGs.
17. 25 Women were trained in Bamboo craft through three months training programme.
18. 40 Women were provided training in Tailoring and Knitting works and they are earning livelihood through these skills.

Discussion

Visible Impact of AAA Programmes

Activities and results under AAA programme are enumerated in Table-1 and 2 in detail and the visible impacts of Applied and Action Anthropology intervention may be summarized as follows:

Self Help Groups

1. Regular saving habits inculcated among members.
2. Several members increased their income adopting income generating activities promoted by the institute.

3. Easy access to financial services ensured.
4. Collective decision- making promoted by institute now institutionalized.
5. SHG members taking up community development works.
6. Women are running Fare Price Shops successfully in the area.

Land and Water Management Programme

1. Waste land converted into farm land helped the villagers in increased crop production.
2. In last Monsoon season, earthen and check-dams constructed by the Institute provided protective irrigation in moisture stress.
3. In canal constructed area some farmers took up two crops this year against one earlier. Some farmers extended their area of Kharif Crops.
4. Tanks constructed by institute helped in fish farming and supplementary irrigation.
5. Boulder and earthen checks proved to be of great help in checking soil erosion in the area.
6. Construction of proper approach road in village Chattauri is of great help in transport and communication to villagers.

Awareness campaign

1. The demonstration effect of transparency and timely payment of wages in the programmes run by TRDI generated high faith and enthusiasm among the tribal community.
2. Migration appears to have lowered down in comparison to previous years due to Creation of wage employment.

Table 1: Showing UNDP and IFAD sponsored programme Activities and Results.

Undp Programme With Regional Research Laboratory, Bhopal)		***Ifad Programme***	
Actions taken	Results	Actions taken	Results
Social survey Jashpur district.	10,169 households	*Selection of Villages and Beneficiaries-*	Shaila,Chirotoli, Chhatauri &Kardana.
Village survey	96 villages	*Rapport Building with Tribal Community*	Oraon, Nagasia & Pahari Korwa
Village resource drawn.	96 villages	*Constitution of GRAM SABHA-*	4 in 4 Natural Map Villages
Formation of Helf Group:	82 SHGs formed and linked with Banks.	Formation of PEC-	4 (1 per Village)

(Contd...)

Six technology packages introduced:. processing	1. Organic Compost 2. Poultry/Piggery/Goat raring 3. Bee keeping and Honey 4. Food processing and NTFP value addition 5. Low cost Nursery 6. Mushroom Cultivation	*Opening of Bank Account of PEC-*	*4* (VCC/CFMC/ WDC)
Technology dissemination	1. Organic compost-236 beds 2. Nadep- 5 units 3. Poultry- 72 units 4. Piggery- 6 families 5. BARI making-1 SHG 6. Detergent powder-1 SHG 7. Fish Farming- 1SHG 8. Bee keeping - 2 units 9. Mushroom cultivation-7 units 10. Irrigation paddle pump-16 units 11. Hybrid He-goat distribution-21Nos. 12. Individual case submitted-117	Constitution of Village wiseTechnical	Committees
Training and workshops :	1. Beekeeping-1 batch of persons 2. Poultry-3 batches of 45 persons 3. Mushroom cultivation batches 4. of 30 persons 5. Vermi- Compost- 200 6. (village level training) 7. Workshops – 78Nos. 8.Village meetings- 173 Nos.	*Regular Monthly* 18 *Meeting -*	

Table 2: Showing PTG *AWAS YOJNA* and World Food Programme sponsored activites and

PTG AWAS YOJNA		***WORLD FOOD PROGRAMME***	
Action Taken	Result	Actions Taken	Results
13 families of Pahari Korwa tribe constructed houses themselves, for the first time in history of their Nomadic life at Manora Block.	13 houses	*Construction of pond (DABRI) –*	5
		Renovation of existing Irrigation Canal–	1
		Construction of Earthen Canal –	1
		Construction of Earthen Bandh-	1
		Construction of Approach Road –	207 m
		Wasteland Development –.	15 Acres
		Formation of SHG	*8,(Male SHG- 2; Female SHG -6)*

References

Bhowmik, P.K.(1966) An Integrated Plan for the Development of Lodhas and other Tribals of Midnapur in West Bengal, Vanyajati, Vol. XIV, No. 2.

Dalton, E.T. (1872) Descriptive Ethnology of Bengal (Reprint) Superintendent, Govt. Printing, Calcutta, 1960.

Majumdar. D.N (1959) Indian Anthropologists in Action, Journal of Social Research, Vol. II, No. 1-2.

Majumdar. D.N (1973) Races and Cultures of India, Asia Publishing House, Bombay, 2nd reprint.

Sachchidanand (1973) Planning, Development and Applied Anthropology in India, Indian Anthropologist, Vol. 3.

Sharma, V.P. (2003) From Hills to Plains-The Story of Pahari Korwa Rehabilitation in Jashpur district, TRDI- Mimeograph.

Sol Tax (1959) Action Anthropology, Journal of Social Research, Vol. II, No. 1-2.

Vidyarthi L.P, (1968) Applied Anthropology in India, [Ed.] Kitab Mahal, Allahabad.

Vidyarthi, L.P, (1972) Problems and Prospects of Tribal Development, Indian Anthropologist, Vol. 2, No. 2.

Vidyarthi. L.P, (1978) Rise of Anthropology in India, Vol. II, Concept Publishing Company, Delhi.

Chapter – 15

Empowerment of tribal women: Challenges and Strategies

The adoption of the 73rd amendment by the Parliament in 1992 had a great revolutionary potential to create genuine democracy at the grassroots village level. It represented a historic opportunity to change the face of rural India. The amendment mandates that resources, responsibility and decision power be devolved from central Government to rural grassroots people through Panchayati Raj Institutions. Their main objective was to realize Mahatma Gandhi's dream of reaching power to the people through Panchayats. In India, the majority of the tribal population depends on forests and forest land for their survival and livelihood. This case study will enlighten you about the Tribal women Health empowerment and Panchayati Raj Institution.

The greatest challenge is to recognize the obstacles that stand in the way of their right to good

Health. To be useful to the family, community and the society, women must be provided with health care facilities. Empowerment would become more relevant if women are educated, better informed and can take rational decisions. It is also necessary to sensitize the other sex towards women. It is important to usher in changes in societal attitudes and perceptions with regard to the role of women in different spheres of life. Adjustments have to be made in traditional gender specific performance of tasks (Sharma 2010).

The study covers **Women empowerment through** various aspects of PRIs in Chhattishgarh and Jharkhand and "Salient Features of the State policy for women health in Chhattisgarh –The policy says-

- Ensure implementation of laws regarding registration of marriages, births and deaths

- To effectively meet the problems of early marriage and infant and maternal mortality
- Provide health training (particularly in reproductive and child health) to women.
- The State would undertake special efforts to meet the nutrient needs especially amongst pregnant and lactating women through education and encouraging participation of women in the planning and delivery of the system
- Expand and intensify access to safe, effective and affordable methods of Family Planning Especially in the rural and tribal areas.

For the following schemes village Panchayat would identify the beneficiaries through Gram Sabha including co-ordination and monitoring of the schemes. Schemes are

1. Participation in the implementation of women and child welfare programmes.
2. Promotion of school health and nutrition programmes.

District Panchayat to coordinate all the activities and schemes of village Panchayat in

1. Preparation of annual action plan
2. Hold monthly meeting of the monitoring committee
3. Provide technical assistance for sanction of village Panchayat related works
4. Participation in the implementation of women and child welfare programmes.
5. Promotion and participation of voluntary organizations in women and child development programmes.
6. Promotion of programmes relating to development of women and children.
7. All the scheme of aganwadi centers. Schemes are:
    - Centrally sponsored ICDS scheme
    - Supplementary nutrition programme
    - Wheat based nutrition programme
    - Kishori Shakti Yojana (Adolescent
    - Girls Scheme)

- Pradhan Mantri Gramodaya Yojana
- MITANIN programme

Government of Chhattisgarh has recently introduced MITANIN programme as women friendly health measures. Altogether 4000 MITANIN were trained by now and are supposed to provide women friendly health services but in lack of their medical kit the program is not being implemented properly in Jashpur district.

Promises made by state in the Policy for women are praiseworthy if they are properly implemented by the government machinery especially through PRI. If the state can provide good health facilities to keep women healthy then they can be empowered further economically through various schemes of development.

Women empowerment through PRI needed steps

It is suggested that local institutions should play a pro-active role to formulate norms and methods to tackle the problem of poverty in rural areas. Though the large number of women related legislations are in place, it is seen that the efficacy of these laws are not satisfactory primarily on account of poor implementation. A major reason for this is the lack of adequate knowledge and awareness regarding these special legislations. Also there is absence of gender sensitivity on part of the functionaries at the Panchayat levels such as law enforcement, police, prosecution, medical profession, education etc. There is a need to give a very high priority to training and capacity building of among the Tribal women especially at Panchayat level.

(a) Women are regaining the sense of self-worth and are no longer willing to take a backseat. They want to be treated with respect and dignity and now hate any ideas or ideology that treat them as a commodity.

(b) They want to take decisions on matters bearing on them.

(c) Women want access to opportunities and resources, without any discrimination, for their economic independence.

(d) They want to be able to influence the social and other changes playing a more active role in nation building activities.

(e) Last but not the least they want total control on their own lives without any undue interference from any quarter.

A substantial number of Scheduled Tribes (STs) women have been elected to the Panchayats.

Therefore, provisions of Social Justice Committee at different levels of Panchayats will have a reasonable positive effect towards their empowerment. It is also true that caste discrimination and atrocities on scheduled castes and Tribes households continue unabated in various states, this is so despite various constitutional provisions and legislative measures. Thus, elected women Panchayat representatives, particularly from ST communities face enormous discriminations in performing their public roles effectively. While continued discrimination in society has a very complex reality, what is really worrisome is that government officials also treat such elected Panchayat representatives with neglect and apathy. Such attitudes and practices further limit the effectiveness of elected Panchayat representatives from ST households. It is therefore, suggested that following action need to be taken up;

- Social Justice Committees should be legislated to be an integral part of each tier of the Panchayat Raj system in all states.
- Ministry of Panchayati Raj, Government of India, can target its BRGF grants to those Gram

  Panchayats and Panchayat Samitis, which are headed by ST elected representatives.
- The Ministries of Panchayati Raj and Rural Development, Government of India, can further utilize BRGF, NREGS, IAY and SGSY resources to undertake specially targeted capacity enhancement programmes for elected Panchayat leaders of women in general and ST women in particular.
- Civil society organizations should be mobilized to join in capacity building of the target population, which among other things could also include literacy skills like rapid reading.

Empowerment of tribal women

In tribal area like Jharkand, economic opportunities for women are scarce while hardships are plentiful. Women often see little hope for themselves or their children to improve their future.

As per NHFS III, Fifty-eight percent of currently married women age 15-49 were employed in the last year, compared with 99 percent of currently married men in the same age group; two-fifths of these women received no payment for their work, and 13 percent were paid only in kind.

Overall, only 47 percent of employed married women earn cash, compared with 87 percent of employed married men. Among married women who work and are paid in cash, 88 percent decide how their earnings will be spent, either alone or together with their husbands. Twenty-four percent of women who work for cash earn about the same or more than their husbands.

Decision making

Married women were asked who makes decisions on their own health care, making large household purchases, making household purchases for daily household needs, and visiting their own family or relatives. About two-thirds of currently married women (60-66%) participate in making each of these decisions. However, only 42 percent of currently married women participate in making all four of these decisions and 20 percent do not participate in making any of the four decisions. Women in nuclear households and women who are employed for cash are more likely to participate in these household decisions. The percent of women who participate in all four decisions increases steadily with age.

Other indicators of women's empowerment

Sixty percent of women have some money that they can decide how to use. The proportion of women with money which they control is highest for women in the highest wealth quintile and women with at least 10 years of education. Only 14 percent of women have a bank or savings account that they themselves use.

Women's knowledge and use of microcredit programmes is fairly limited. Only 26 percent of women have heard of any microcredit programme in the area and only 2 percent have ever used one.

Only 51 percent of women are allowed to go by themselves to the market, only 47 percent are allowed to go by themselves to a health facility, and only 40 percent are allowed to go by themselves to places outside their own village or community (data not shown in tables).

Overall, 37 percent of women are allowed to go alone to all three of these places. Older women, scheduled-tribe women, women in nuclear households, and those with 10 or more years of education have more freedom of movement than other women.

Gender-role attitudes

Half of women in Jharkhand believe it is justifiable for a husband to beat his wife under some specific circumstances. Women are most likely to say wife beating is justified if a woman shows disrespect for her in-laws (32%), or if she neglects the house or children or she argues with him (each 30%). Men are less likely than women to agree; 33 percent of men say wife beating is justified in some specific circumstances, including 19 percent of men who believe arguing with her husband is justification for wife beating. Even among women and men who have completed at least 10 years of schooling, one in five agree that a husband is justified in beating his wife for one or more specified reasons.

More than 8 in 10 women and men agree that a woman is justified in refusing to have sex with her husband for each of the following reasons: if she knows he has a sexually transmitted disease, if she knows he has intercourse with other women, or if she is tired or not in the mood. (National Family Health Survey (NFHS-3) India 2005-06)

Gender socialization

India has traditionally been a male dominated society. There is a strong son preference in most parts of India, and girls tend to be discriminated against by their families. It is not enough, therefore, to highlight adolescence in general; a larger focus of the girl child also must be addressed. Demographic trends indicate deep-rooted gender discrimination. Discrimination begins with female feticide and prenatal sex determination.

Education and employment

There is visible and strong gender discrimination in education. The 1998–99 National Family Health Survey-2 (NFHS-2) reported that among young female adolescents (ages 10–14 years), 67 percent attended school. The corresponding figure for male adolescents was 80.2 percent. There was a sharp decline in the proportion of female adolescents (ages 15–17) attending the school. Only 40.3 percent attended school compared to 57.7 percent of their male counterparts. In rural areas, only 32.7 percent of female adolescents (ages 15–17) attended school compared with 60.5 percent of female adolescents in urban areas. In India, the minimum age for working in any factory or mine is 14 years and the minimum age for government jobs is 18 years, but use of young child laborers is quite prevalent. The Planning Commission of India estimated about 20 million child laborers in the year 2000. In 1998, the National Survey Organization found that approximately 6 percent of female and male children ages 5–14 years are working in rural areas and about 5 percent are working in urban areas. They are primarily involved in work in the non-formal sectors, which is not visible and goes unreported. The 1998–1990 National Sample Survey Organization (NSSO) showed that 48.9 percent of the female work force in the 10–14 year-old age group was involved in the self-employed, non-agricultural sector.

Marriage

Indian culture promotes universal marriage. Of importance to ARH is the traditional young marriage age of girls—referred to as early marriage. The national average age at marriage for women in India is 16.4 years, although there are vast regional variations. NFHS-2 reports that in states like Rajasthan, Bihar, Uttar Pradesh, Madhya Pradesh, and Andhra Pradesh, girls are married at around age. According to NFHS-2, about one-third of women were married by age 15 and two-thirds (64.6 percent) by age 18.13 Marriage by age 18 is most prevalent in Rajasthan, Bihar, Uttar Pradesh, Madhya Pradesh, and Andhra Pradesh, where nearly 80 percent of girls are married by age 18. In these states, almost one-half of the girls are married by the time they are 15 years old. Nationwide, the district-based Rapid Household Surveys (RHSs) found that in 145 of the 504 districts in India, one-half of women were married before age 18. In some districts, the proportion married by age 18 was as high as 75 percent.

Table 3.10.1

Adolescent Population (15-24) (000's)	***2000***	***2005***	***2010***	***2015***	***2020***
Males	98.9	107.1	112.9	115.2	110.0
Females	91.2	99.4	105.3	108.1	104.2
2. Level of Education (%)	1993 (M)	1993 (F)	1999 (M)	1999 (F)	
No Education	20.9	47.8	16.8	38.4	
Primary Incomplete	7.5	6.2	7.5	6.8	
Primary Complete/Some Secondary	16.7	13.8	18.7	16.2	
Secondary Complete and Higher	54.9	32.2	57.1	38.6	
3. Pregnancy Outcomes (000's)	2000	2005	2010	2015	2020
Total Pregnancies	20.2	22.1	23.5	24.2	23.6
Birth	14.9	16.4	17.4	18.0	17.6
Abortions	2.1	2.3	3.2	3.6	3.5
Miscarriages	3.0	3.3	3.5	3.6	3.5
4. Unmet Need (%)	1993	1999			
Total Unmet Need (15-19)	30.4	27.1			
Total Unmet Need (20-24)	27.9	24.4			

3.10.2 Pre- Conception & Pre- Natal Diagnostic Techniques (PCPNDT) Act.

In Jharkhand some districts still have a healthy sex ratio as compared to the National average Table 2 also shows the decline in the ratio which is alarming and has to be taken cognizance of. Necessary and timely steps need to be undertaken before the situation starts damaging the social fabric of the state.

Jharkhand is a state with a tough geographical terrain and predominance of tribal population. The rural sex ratio (Table 1), though at a respectable figure, is showing a declining trend. This coupled with out-migration of the girls to other states for economic reasons surely rings a bell of alarm. The situation warrants for intensive and specific interventions to reverse the falling sex ratio graph.

Table 3: Child sex ratio in the age group 0-6 years by residence: 1991 & 2001

	2001			*1991*			*Difference (2001-1991)*		
	Total	*Rural*	*Urban*	*Total*	*Rural*	*Urban*	*Total*	*Rural*	*Urban*
Jharkhand	965	973	930	979	985	950	-14	-13	-20

Table 2: District-wise Child Sex Ratio in 1991 and 2001

Districts	*1991*	*2001*	*Difference*
Garhwa	969	962	-7
Palamu	982	967	-15
Chatra	1001	975	-26
Hazaribagh	978	966	-12
Koderma	989	975	-14
Giridih	993	978	-15
Deoghar	987	973	-14
Godda	984	978	-6
Sahibganj	963	973	+10
Pakur	987	964	-23
Dumka	984	977	-7
Dhanbad	966	951	-15
Bokaro	982	950	-32
Ranchi	968	961	-7
Lohardaga	984	945	-39
Gumla	988	976	-12
West Singhbhum	987	969	-18
East Singhbhum	958	941	-17

Situational analysis of all the institutions/organizations in the state functioning in the following areas: GCC - Genetic Counseling Centres; GL – Genetic Laboratories; GC - Genetic Clinics; USC/IC - Ultrasound Clinics/ Imaging Centres; JAGCC/GL/GC- Jointly as Genetic Counseling Centres/ Gen. Labs./Gen. Clinics; MC(V) - Mobile Clinics (Vehicles); OB/IVFC/ IC- Other bodies/IVF Centres/Infertility Centres. Line listing and consequent involvement, through a consultative process, of all the organizations/ institutions/bodies having a stake in the issue.

Number of bodies registered under PC &PNDT Act 1994 (As on March, 2005)

Jharkhand (all the bodies registered in Jharkhand are USC/ICs)	Number of Bodies registered
	233

Conclusion

A woman needs to be physically healthy so that she is able to take challenges of equality. But it is sadly lacking in a majority of women especially in the rural areas. They have unequal access to basic health resources and lack adequate counseling. Various development programmes have been implemented by the government to protect tribal women from social injustice and all forms of exploitation and to uplift their standard of living. Increasingly large amount is being spent, over the years, both by the Central and State govt. for the development of the Tribal area but the result is far from satisfaction level including Health services. Tribal women need to be trained to play their active role in Panchayati Raj Institution and avail the benefits. There is a need to have capacity building Initiatives and training, orientation in Panchayati Raj Institutions (PRIs), Accountability & Transparency, Development of Model Gram Panchayats, Panchayat Extension of Scheduled Area Act (PESA) and Backward Regions Grant Fund" should be ensure that its benefits reaches to the Gram Panchayat level.

References

1. District Health Action Plans for 2010–2011, 11-12. Jashpur, CG, Unpublished document, n.d.
2. Health and Family Welfare Department, Operational guidelines for implementation of Janani Suraksha Yojana., n.d. http://angul.nic.in/JSY.pdf Accessed 6 June 2009.
3. Ministry of Health and Family Welfare, 'JANANI SURAKSHA YOJANA: Guidelines for Implementation., n.d. 4. http://www.mohfw.nic.in/layout_09-06.pdf Accessed 6 June 2009.

4. Sharma, V.P. Health Empowerment of Women in Jharkhand, Social Modernity: Asian Journal of Social Science,Vol. I N0. 1-2,June-December 2010, pp. 60-66, Ranchi.
5. Sharma, Vijay Prakash. Promoting Institutional Deliveries in Tribal Areas: The Role of Janani Suraksha Yojna (JSY), Journal of Social Research, Vol. 36-39: 1&2, pp. 46-52, September 2012 - March 2013. Ranchi.
6. Society of Tribal Women for Development (STWFD), Impact of Bottom up Planning under PRIs and Women participation therein in the States of Madhya Pradesh, Orissa, Chhattisgarh, Gujarat.
7. Jharkhand and Maharashtra, Report submitted to Planning Commission. Government of India, ND.

Index

T

U

V

W

Y